The best value career book ever

THE BEST VALUE

Career

BOOK EVER

Ken Langdon & John Middleton

infinite ideas

Careful now

We want you to have a stimulating and rewarding career but we're not going to go out there and get it for you. You're a grown up now so it's up to you to take responsibility for your own future. The tips in here need to be combined with effort on your part in order to work; if at first you don't succeed, have a think about whether it was your approach rather than our advice that was at fault, and then have another go. We know you're up to the challenge, so get out there and grab the career you want.

Although the contents of this book were checked at the time of going to press, the World Wide Web is constantly changing. This means the publisher and author cannot guarantee the contents of any of the websites mentioned in the book.

Acknowledgements

Infinite Ideas would like to thank the following authors for their contributions to this book: Rob Bevan, Nikki Cartwright, Penny Ferguson, Andrew Holmes, Ken Langdon, John Middleton, Jon Smith, Elisabeth Wilson and Tim Wright

The right of the authors to be identified as the author of this book has been asserted in accordance with the Copyright, Designs and Patents Act 1988.

First published in 2007 by
The Infinite Ideas Company Limited
36 St Giles
Oxford
OX1 3LD
United Kingdom
www.infideas.com

A CIP catalogue record for this book is available from the British Library

ISBN 13: 978-1-904902-87-4
ISBN 10: 1-904902-87-1

Brand and product names are trademarks or registered trademarks of their respective owners.

Text design and typeset by Baseline Arts Ltd, Oxford
Cover design by Cylinder
Printed in India

Brilliant ideas

Brilliant features

Each chapter of this book is designed to provide you with an inspirational idea that you can read quickly and put into practice straight away.

Throughout you'll find three features that will help you to get right to the heart of the idea:

■ *Here's an idea for you* Give it a go – right here, right now – and get an idea of how well you're doing so far.

■ *Defining ideas* Words of wisdom from masters and mistresses of the art, plus some interesting hangers-on.

■ *How did it go?* If at first you do succeed try to hide your amazement. If, on the other hand, you don't this is where you'll find a Q and A that highlights common problems and how to get over them.

Introduction

If you've picked up this book then we assume you're already interested in your working life as more than a means to an end. Having said that, some people are prepared to put more into their careers than others. Some of us will simply want to find out how to get the most out of the jobs we're in and progress quietly up the ranks, while at the other end of the scale others want to know how to get from university to the boardroom in the shortest possible time. While we can't guarantee to make this happen we do have some fantastic ideas to help fuel your ambitions and we hope everyone reading this book will find some new, exciting and inspirational tips.

This is probably not the first book on careers that you've read, but we hope that it will prove the most innovative. While other books may only focus on one particular aspect of working life (such as interview technique) we cover the whole range, from crafting that first CV through managing your own team and beyond. We've also included ideas about balancing your work and home life, setting up your own business and dealing with redundancy. Our editors have consulted dozens of authors to bring you the very best career ideas so that now you need look no further than this book for success secrets to last you from leaving school until retirement.

We know you're not superhuman, so all our ideas are achievable if you're prepared to put in the time and effort. Our authors are not management gurus who have lost touch with the realities of working life, but real people who have created the ideas through their own personal experiences whilst trying to build their careers. And just in case you do have problems the first time you try out an idea we've included a question and answer section at the end of each chapter, where our authors suggest solutions to problems related to the idea.

Don't feel you need to try all the tips in order. This book has been designed so that you can dip into it anywhere, any time. If you have a particular problem you need to sort out – difficult colleagues, overwork, underpay or an imminent interview – then turn straight to the relevant idea to sort it out. Other ideas will give you more general advice for all round career happiness. Above all we hope you enjoy reading the book. A great career takes effort but if you work hard, relax well and make sure you do something that interests you you're halfway there.

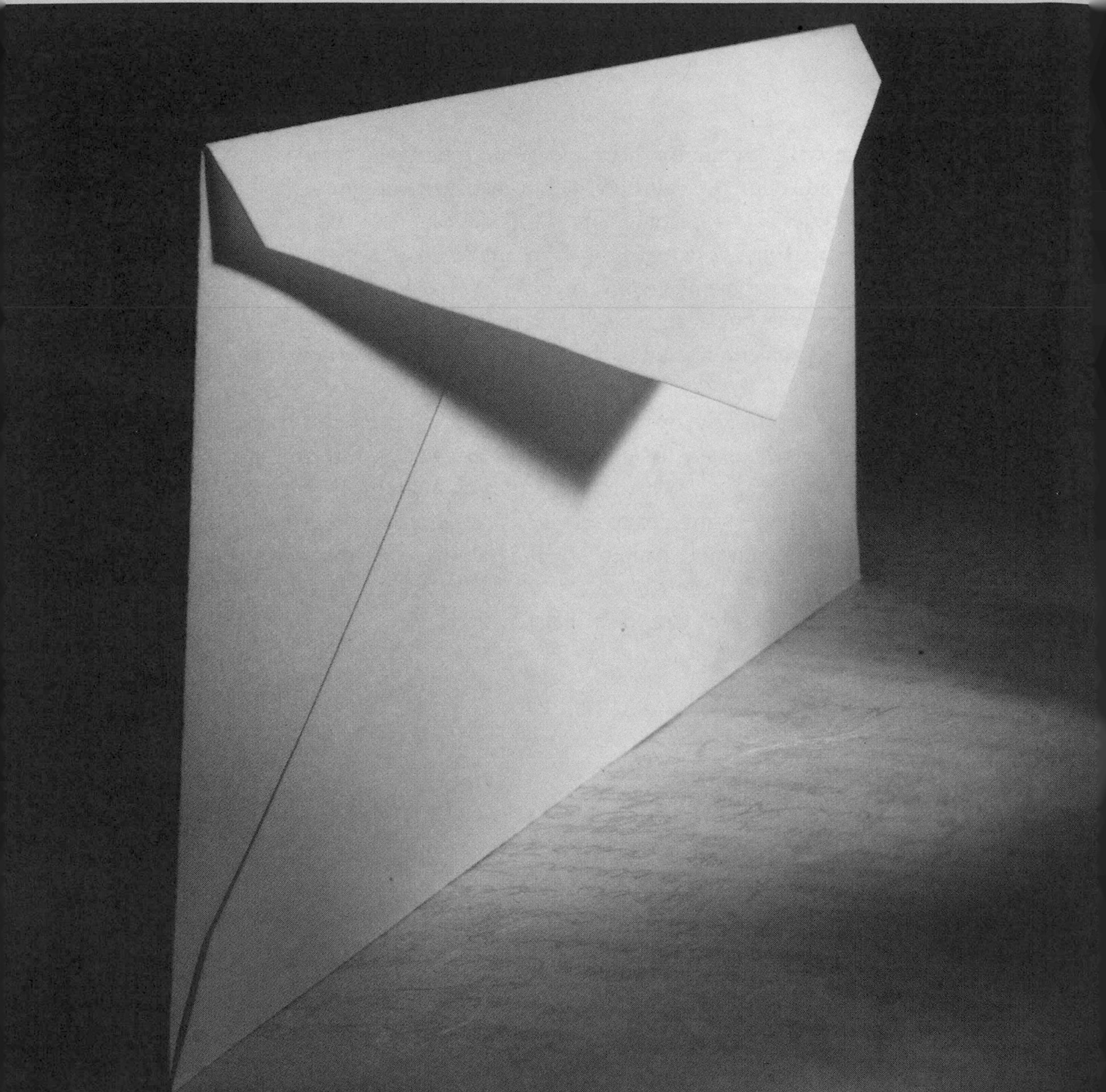

1

Manage the brand called You

A unique selling point will make you stand out from the crowd. So, what makes you so special?

What particular combination of skills and experience might give you an edge over others going for the same job?

'It's this simple: you are a brand. You are in charge of your brand. There is no single path to success. And there is no one right way to create the brand called You. Except this: Start today. Or else.'

That's a quote from Tom Peters, probably the world's best known (and best paid) management guru, in an article called 'The Brand Called You: You Can't Move Up If You Don't Stand Out' that he wrote for *Fast Company* magazine in August 1997. In a nutshell, the article proposed that we should manage our career as though it were a brand. Peters proposed that like a classic marketing brand, our personal brand value can rise or fall depending on how well we nurture and manage our brand and how well we perform in the marketplace.

Take England footballer Wayne Rooney, for example. Football commentators reckon that his performances during the Euro 2004 tournament increased his value in the transfer market fourfold. Imagine how much more he would have been worth if he hadn't tripped over his own boot and broken a bone in his foot!

Here's an idea for you...

Ask yourself the following deceptively simple question to help you define your brand: What do I want to be famous for? Then ask yourself what needs to happen next in order for you to get closer to your chosen brand identity.

But this isn't just a concept to apply to people with a high media profile. You may cringe at the thought of being 'a brand called You' or 'Chief Executive of Me', but behind this clodhopping language rests a new truth about what lays ahead for everyone looking to change jobs.

To put it bluntly, getting a new job isn't the challenge. Finding the right job is, however. Whether you're contemplating an internal or external move, you need to make sure that it keeps your career moving in an upward trajectory. Choose the right employer and that can increase your brand value. Choose the wrong employer and you can do lasting damage to your earning potential.

So, what can we do to protect our careers?

ACTIVELY MANAGE YOUR CAREER

I can sympathise if reading this stuff is making you feel like a lie-down, but please don't be like most of your colleagues, who probably manage their careers on the hoof. The trouble is, the general assumption seems to be that performing well in a given job is all that matters. In other words, look after your job and somehow your career will take care of itself. Not true. Building a long and successful career requires a 'planned maintenance' mentality. Don't assume that combining patience with a dollop of opportunism will do the trick – bugger all comes to they who wait. Or to quote my favourite Chinese proverb: 'A peasant must stand a long time on a hillside with his mouth wide open before a roast duck flies in.'

KEEP YOUR HANDS ON THE WHEEL

Don't entrust your career to anybody. Don't rely on the company's Management Development Manager or VP-Succession Planning to look after your interests – they have other fish to fry. And don't rely on your current boss to look after your best interests. Now I admit that I may be doing them a grave disservice, but all too many managers are very happy to keep their good people for as long as they possibly can.

Here's the acid test: has your boss ever said anything to you along the lines of 'I'm concerned that you're not spending enough time planning your next job move. You should be keeping an eye out for the right opportunity. Oh, and start networking more'? Paradoxically, if your boss has been saying that to you, it's probably because they think you're rubbish at your job and they're desperate to shuffle you off the premises.

AIM HIGH

Finally, don't imagine that the skills, knowledge and experience that got you where you are today will be sufficient to propel you where you want to be in the future. Seek out opportunities to acquire new skills, become a voracious learner and develop career purpose. People with a vision of their future and goals linked to that vision are far more likely to succeed than those who don't.

'In a nutshell, the key to success is identifying unique modules of talent within you and then finding the right arena in which to use them.'
WARREN BENNIS, author and social philosopher

Defining idea...

'You don't have an old-fashioned résumé anymore! You've got a marketing brochure for brand You.'
TOM PETERS, management guru

Defining idea...

How did
it go?

Q   I'm struggling to put this idea into practice. Can you provide a few practical pointers on how I can build my brand value?

A   *Personal brand building happens over months and years rather than days and weeks. You'll need to commit quite a bit of time and energy to the process. In a magazine article, Tom Peters gave five tips:*

1. *Find a mentor: Time was when mentors used to pick their protégés, these days, protégés are likely to be picking their mentors.*

2. *Look the part: Dress in a style that suits your job, and which matches people's expectations.*

3. *Become an active member of your professional association: It will increase your professional know-how and help you build an impressive set of contacts.*

4. *Specialise: Be the person that everybody turns to when the budget needs checking, or the computer goes wrong, or when people want a good listener.*

√   5. *Develop your presentation skills.*

Q   These all seem like useful short-term steps to take, but what about in the longer term?

√   A   *The most important thing is to have a vision: think hard about your goals and how you're going to achieve them.*

2

Stop the world, I want to play the banjo

We all fantasise about chucking in the day job from time to time. Let's look at some of the issues involved in turning comforting fantasy into gritty reality.

Personally I blame Felicity Kendall. When the actress and former Rear of the Year appeared in the BBC comedy series 'The Good Life' back in the 1970s, she gave physical form to a widely held yearning for simple, corporation-free living.

So what is downshifting? It's been defined as the deliberate decision to simplify and enrich your life by balancing work and home life, reducing levels of financial commitment, etc., at the expense of your income.

As I say, the idea is not new. Over the past ten years or so, the movement has gained a new lease of life against a backdrop of marked changes in the world of

Here's an idea for you...

If you've moved to a cheaper area as part of your downsizing exercise, it helps if you have a strategy for bonding with the natives. Not paying attention to this side of the equation can cause a measure of resentment with the local population, particularly as the properties that you and other downshifters have bought outright could well be the same houses that the more aspirational village locals are looking to 'upshift' into.

employment and employability. To more and more people feeling stressed out by a high-pressure work life, it's become a bit of a fantasy to considering swapping corporately induced misery for a simpler, more satisfying way of life.

And some have turned the fantasy into reality. Wander around a typical Cornish village these days and you're likely to chance upon former bank employees now running bed and breakfasts, not to mention ex-stockbrokers who have taken up painting (or, worse still, the accordion).

From a financial perspective, the 'ex-' and 'former' in the previous sentence are significant. Downshifting implicitly requires the cashing in of resources we've already acquired, and so it's less suited to those of us in the early stages of our career and on the lower rungs of the property ladder.

Of course, the decision whether to downshift is not merely a financial decision. It's more like a life decision with financial and social consequences. Here are some key questions that any potential downshifter needs to face:

- Are you really prepared to sacrifice part of your income for a better quality of life?

- Have you tried mapping out a budget for your downsized life to decide if it's feasible? Are you really prepared to go without those restaurant meals, those nights at the opera, etc.?

- Where's your downsized income going to come from? Do you need to negotiate reduced hours with your current employers, or are you looking for a completely new income stream? Are you planning to release some capital by selling your old place?

Defining idea...

'*Let's not get carried away, though. We still have a long way to go before we catch up with the Ancient Greeks' ideals of self-development through leisure, recreation and education for its own sake. The "golden mean", they believed, lay between wealth and poverty. It's a long haul. But we have made a start.*'
JUDY JONES, co-author of *Getting a Life*, writing in *Resurgence* magazine

At the heart of a successful downshifting move is a reality-centred understanding of the life and financial changes it will involve. If you are truly prepared to take on all that downshifting entails, you could be heading towards a more satisfying, less financially dependent future. However, it's not for the faint-hearted. Dewy-eyed fantasists need not apply.

Defining idea...

'*Civilisation, in the real sense of the term, consists not in the multiplication, but in the deliberate and voluntary reduction of wants.*'
MAHATMA GANDHI

7

How did it go?

Q **I've decided to trade in the corporate suit for a downsized life. I just hope the new life suits me.**

A   *When you say 'me', is this your decision alone, or would you have to negotiate with others? For example, relocating from London to an ex-miner's cottage in Wales might satisfy your yearning for the rural idyll, but your kids might be less enthusiastic about leaving their friends and social life behind.*

Q **What if a life of lentils and low income turns out not to be for me?**

A   *You would do well to have an exit strategy just in case downshifting doesn't suit you. What would you do? Your urban career trajectory may lie in tatters after two years of sheep rearing. Many employers would be sceptical about your willingness and ability to pick up your old career where you left off.*

So how could you convince them that you've retained your old skill set? It would help if you could point to some recent consultancy that you've undertaken in your field, or perhaps some relevant training.

3

Nothing can go wrong, because nothing is planned

In days gone by, project management was the business of engineers who had techniques to control complex sets of activities. Nowadays, careerists need to treat a fluid list of activities as a project. Make sure you don't have one arm tied behind your back before you start.

The old image of organisations comprising separate functions operating on their own is giving way to cross-functional teams, and it's a good career move to manage at least one.

Taking on a high-profile project, particularly a change project, once again gives you exposure high and wide in the organisation.

A lot of projects are doomed to fail before they start because the manager doesn't recognise the need to define and manage activities as a project. Here's the holy trinity of rules for announcing and managing a project:

Here's an idea for you...

Find something difficult that needs to be done, some major change that the organisation needs to make. Perhaps your boss hasn't thought of it or has thought it too tough, but he or she would be happy to take the credit for it. Offer to manage it, and deliver.

■ The timescale from start to finish is more than a month, often a lot longer.

■ There is more than one function involved.

■ You do not have direct authority over all the people and resources needed.

If these three elements are in place go to your boss and propose that she becomes the sponsor of the project. Outline your vision for how things will look once the project is complete. Make sure the timing is right. Before you announce your project, test for 'management initiative overload'. This is a syndrome that haunts many organisations that have too many initiatives going on simultaneously, none of which ever gets completed. Don't start something that you can't finish. Never fight a battle you can't win. You're going to run it high profile so it's got to be successful. If your vision is bold and useful enough your boss may cancel someone else's pet project to divert resources to your new one. This is excellent careermanship. If it happens, make sure you are the first person to sympathise with the thwarted colleague, 'but what could I do, you know what she's like when she has the bit between her teeth?'

KICK-START IT BY THINKING THE PROJECT THROUGH TO THE END

The key to the beginning of the plan is assessing the chances of success. Look for strong driving forces that, for example, close a competitive gap, or gain competitive edge. They are strong if they translate easily into sales growth and so on. Restraining forces include people's natural resistance to change and their current workload. Remember, most projects aimed at improving the working environment actually create more work for people. Weigh up these forces. If the risk, to business and career, is sensible, go for it.

Finally think about roughly how much resource you will need and how available it is likely to be. Negotiate for this now, before you volunteer to take on the task.

'At one time people were expected to simply get on with their job and not worry about the "whole" picture. These days people have to understand the whole of the business to ensure that they can work in a cross matrix way and are able to move swiftly across the business to areas of greatest need.'
JOHN A. HART, HR Director, Powergen

Defining idea...

CHECK THE STAKEHOLDERS

Make a list of all the stakeholders, people who will in some way be affected by the project – this will be not only your key team members but also your customers and possibly your suppliers. You've got to get them all on board sooner or later, so make sure the list is complete. Think about how much authority your sponsor has, and wriggle out of any project where the sponsor is totally incompetent at getting his own way, or hated sufficiently for people to want anything he touches to fail.

How did it go?

Q   I worked out a plan to change something very important in our organisation, went through the resource requirement and went to my boss for a decision. She was very enthusiastic about the promised results, but wouldn't give me all the resources I need. How do I get out of the situation where I've got a commitment that I know I can't achieve with the resources allowed?

A   *That's bad. If you'd told me earlier I would have suggested that you leak elements of the project bit by bit, checking that everyone thought the use of the resource was worthwhile. You could have built in a lot of contingency resource so that when your boss cut it down, as they always do, it didn't wreck the chances of the project working. As it is, I think you need to decide when the project will be looking at its most promising and destined for success; at that time use a presentation of where you are now to find another opportunity somewhere else in the company. Don't hang around until it actually goes over the cliff.*

Q   I'm trying to get the job of managing a project to relocate three small facilities into one new office block. My boss says that I should go on our internal project management course. This takes up quite a lot of time. Should I do it or leave the relocation to someone else?

A   *You've answered your own question I think. Someone's going to do it and potentially deliver very high-profile success. The person who does it will have to talk to everyone! To be honest I think relocation is much easier than people make out. The difficulty is not the mechanics of the move, but the politics of where everyone ends up – and that's great fun. I do think project management training is very useful nowadays. I'd find the time.*

4

You are totally responsible for you

It is a great mistake to think that anyone is as interested in your career as you are. Once you are past first-line management, you have to work out where you want to go and how to get there. Use the annual appraisal to get your boss's agreement to what you want to do.

Give your boss an easy time.

Even if you have a very open relationship with your boss the annual appraisal is vital to your career plan. Do the preparation and preferably do it better than your boss. No one is as dedicated to your career as you. No one is as good as you at knowing what skills you need. Help your boss along by working all that out before the appraisal interview.

Get yourself ready and in the right frame of mind by asking yourself these questions:

- What value have you added to your job?
- Where is it that you would like to go?
- What do you need to do to get there?
- Why should your boss support these plans? What's in it for her?

Lots of managers like to broadcast the fact that they don't really take the appraisal system seriously, that they have done no prep and that the whole thing will be over in twenty minutes. Encourage this thinking, agree that it's a ritual and that only the salary review has any significance. And then go home and do the preparation assiduously.

Answering these questions before an appraisal interview will mean that you will make the most productive use of this great opportunity to talk about yourself. Remember, this is your career, not your organisation's. Take ownership of that career and impress your boss with your motivation and determination. If you've got a clear idea of your career strategy you'll be much more impressive than an employee who agrees to whatever is suggested and has no proposals of his or her own. More or less writing your own appraisal should make life easier for your boss as well.

SELL THEM ON YOUR IDEAS FOR YOUR CAREER

While your career is your own, remember also that you are a team player in an organisation with its own aims and strategies. It is an entity in its own right and this must be reflected in the way you express yourself during an appraisal interview. That is why the question 'why should your boss support these plans?' is so important. You need to be able to prove that you are a valuable asset to the organisation and that if it invests in you, you will become even more valuable. Start from the very top. What words can you use that link your activities with the fundamental vision or mission of the organisation you work for? Then come down through the division and eventually to your boss.

Another key thing to remember at appraisal time is that the person interviewing you is not an unidentifiable member of the corporate zoo; she is in fact a person with her own ambitions and career plans. Be sensitive to this. Do not alienate your boss by appearing to be more ambitious, more clued up, more prepared to succeed than her (even if it's true). What you are trying to do is to get your boss to adopt your plan, which you present subtly and sensitively, because she can see how it is going to make her look good. You do not need to ram this down her throat; she can work it out.

'Always take every opportunity offered to receive training. Give careful thought to your training needs before any appraisal interview.'
GEORGE PAUL, Chairman, Norwich Union

Defining idea...

A little flattery can go a long way. If you're feeling particularly outrageous, you could even suggest that one day you hope to attain the giddy heights of responsibility that your boss has (although this one takes a firm jaw, a straight face and a very sincere stance to get away with it).

You may already have a job purpose statement or job description agreed with your employer. If not, the appraisal is a splendid opportunity to define your own. If you already have a job purpose statement, expand on it to ensure that your future career aspirations are as easy as possible to achieve.

How did it go?

Q **I did the preparation thoroughly, went in and showed it. My boss said I was being too inflexible, that I had prejudged the result of the interview and that she had some ideas for me as well. How do I recover?**

A *Yes, you have a boss who prepares carefully as well. You probably hit her with too many ideas and surprises at once. It's not easy, but having decided the route you want to take, you needed to help her to feel that actually it was all her idea. The situation you are in now means that you are going to have to take her suggestions very seriously at least for the present. Next time talk to her during the two to three weeks before your career discussion. Suggest some possibilities, leak one or two aspirations, and thank and congratulate her when she comes to a conclusion that suits you.*

Q **I wrote my job description and it went down well with my boss. It does mean that a number of people in the team need to change how they work with me. How do I tell them about that without getting up their noses?**

A *Don't. Get your boss to do it. In fact, encourage your boss to launch the new way of doing things as though it was all his idea. That way any unhappiness in the team will be aimed at him.*

Q **Appraisal, what appraisal? What do you do if the organisation has no formal appraisal system?**

A *Pretend it does. Organise regular meetings with your boss and make sure you discuss your performance and your career with them. Hey, if you keep away from the dreaded 'appraisal' word you could be the only person in the organisation using such meetings to their advantage.*

16

5

Acting up

The use of assessment centres to evaluate potential employees is widespread. Don't think you can't prepare for them.

As with any interview, have in mind the precise impression you want to leave behind. The clearer you have this impression in your mind, the better will be the filter through which you pass the decisions you have to make during the exercises.

Be a contributing member of the group but ration your contributions to times when they move the group forward. Be prepared to compromise and try not to go out on a limb unless you're absolutely sure you're right.

Here's an idea for you...

Think about the impression you want to leave behind when the interviews are over. Write this down so that you have it really well expressed. A good example is, 'I don't make rash decisions.' This will tend to lower the risks that you take at the centre. Now practise it. You can do this in normal meetings in your current job or you can ask other people to role-play with you. Then ask for feedback on the impression you made to see how accurately it mirrors your plan.

OK, TURN OVER YOUR PAPERS

Find out as much as you can about what the assessment centre will involve. Typically, you and the others will be given a group exercise where a team has to discuss a situation and come up with decisions about what to do next. The exercises will generally be relevant to the sort of job you're going for. If you're going for a sales job it will almost certainly involve a customer situation. If you're to become a team leader for the first time it's likely to involve handling a difficult team member. In all cases, look for an opportunity to suggest to the team how it might structure the discussion.

There are some basic communication rules for group discussion:

■ It's easy to think that your contribution to a group discussion occurs when you're speaking. In fact in these group discussions it's often the person who says least who looks best. Listen to what people are saying, rather than spending your whole time preparing your next brilliant epigram.

■ Don't interrupt people to get your point in. It's bad practice and rude, but you'll be amazed how much it happens.

- Look for occasions where you can support something that someone has just said: 'That was a really helpful contribution, Penny; thank you.'

- When someone has said something that you think has merit but needs more explanation, don't jump in and take it in your own direction. It's much better teamwork to ask them a clarifying question.

- When you know something about the group, you should be able to find an opportunity where, because of their background and experience, some people should be in a better position than others to make a contribution. It's very good team technique to invite such individuals to comment. This demonstrates skills in group discussion leadership: 'You know about the production side, Ellen. What do you think?'

'It is the province of knowledge to speak and is the priviledge of wisdom to listen'
OLIVER WENDELL HOLMES, nineteenth-century US author

Defining idea...

WAIT TILL YOU CAN SEE THE WHITES OF THEIR EYES

Try not to jump into the discussion too early. It can be very effective to sit and listen hard to what's being said, asking questions and bringing people in appropriately.

Then form your view. Towards the end you can then give a comprehensive summary of the points that have been made and give your view or support someone else's view. With luck you may be instrumental in helping the group to come to an agreed decision.

THEY'RE ROLE-PLAYING; YOU'RE BEING YOURSELF

Try to look at role-play exercises in this way. If you're the salesperson and that's your job, then you're not role-playing; you're carrying out your function. Use the preparation time they give you. We know it's obvious, but do read the scenario meticulously. Generally, there's not much padding in the briefing; all the sentences and phrases are significant. So try not to miss anything. Try to connect the briefing to a real situation you've been in. It may not be that similar, but anything a bit like it can be helpful in making it feel real.

You're not on your own. If there's time, speak to other people at the centre to see what they make of the briefing. Ask the interviewers if you feel there is a piece of information that in real life you would have. They may decline to tell you, but it's worth trying. Take some deep breaths before you start. Go as slowly as you can. The temptation is to say too much too fast. Use open questions and try to relax. That's all there is to it.

At the end of an assessment centre session, the organisers have a lot of valuable data about you. Ask them for feedback. In most cases they'll give you it if you ask, but possibly not if you don't.

Q   **I have a colleague who's been to an assessment centre. Would it help me if I got her to talk about it and tell me what went on? Is it a good idea when you're at the centre to phone people in the outside world?**

How did it go?

A   *It will probably help to discuss your colleague's experience. Get her to talk about the feedback sessions as well as about what she had to do. Yes, it's a great idea to get help from outside – that's what you'd do in real life.*

Q   **If I don't take much part in the early part of the discussion, won't that make the others look more like leaders than I will?**

A   *No. Look at how good leaders handle group discussions and planning meetings. They generally start by asking the group lots of questions. Perhaps you shouldn't stay entirely quiet, but during the early stages try to limit yourself to asking questions and bringing others in.*

6

Know what to say to whom

A meteoric careerist can't have too much exposure to top people. Think hard about extending your senior contacts.

You happen to be in the lift with your Chairman, or a senior executive of a major customer. Make sure you know what you would say to them.

Most of us in such a situation are like rabbits caught in the headlights and blow this short window of time with small talk. There is a clue here for the careerist. But it's not just about the Chairman.

You can expand on this by dropping in on anyone. Hewlett Packard used to have a useful slogan, 'managing by wandering around'. It was a neat way of reminding managers that part of their job was to be around and meet people by chance as well as in formal meetings. I extended this to 'selling by wandering around', which meant using the same technique to cruise around customer premises making new, and preferably high-level, contacts. 'Cultivating your career by wandering around?' It's not as snappy but that doesn't mean that it doesn't work.

Here's an idea for you...

If, for example, you know your boss's diary you'll know when she is going to be talking to a person you would like to meet. First, prepare. If you did get the opportunity, what would you say? So, you know what you would say; now engineer the opportunity to say it. The best way is simply to breeze in. 'Oh, I'm sorry I didn't realise...' 'That's all right,' says your boss, 'Come in and meet Lord so-and-so.' She will probably add more in terms of a quick description of what you do for the organisation, and that is your moment. 'As a matter of fact, Lord so-and-so, I've been thinking that we ought to have a brief word on...' Brilliant: a new contact – put it in the address book.

PLAN YOUR ABSENCES

Try to be in the office at the same time as your boss. After all, in your absence she might give an interesting and potentially rewarding opportunity to someone else. You need to know her diary so that you can plan your absences at times when she won't notice you're not there.

The clincher for how vital it is to know your boss's diary is that you will know when she is definitely far away. Believe me, there is nothing more embarrassing than being caught nosing around in someone else's files.

Obviously you want high-level exposure to things that go well. You also want cover against being held responsible for something going wrong. Short-sighted people with moderate ambitions keep a detailed record of their activities with a note of the people who supported them on the way. The more ambitious person with her eye on the big picture does it in such a way that the record can prove that others were completely responsible if it goes wrong. Don't forget to have a shredder handy if all goes well, though. It wouldn't do for you to enable someone else to take the glory.

'It's not how you play the game, but who you get to take the blame' goes the rhyme. This is the business version of the Olympic spirit. If you're involved with high-level operations it's generally not a good idea to be closely associated with failure. Stay clear of the firing line unless there are massive Brownie points for effort as opposed to achievement.

'There is no stronger way of building a career than "working the corridors".'
RICHARD HUMPHREYS, serial chairman

Defining idea...

There is another way of looking at this if the cock-up is really huge. A person in charge of a substantial development project spent £50 million of his company's money on it and was, towards the end, powerless to prevent it having no impact on the business at all. The entire sum was completely wasted. Asked into his boss's office he pre-empted the inevitable by saying that he knew he was there to be fired. 'No way,' said his boss, a very aware woman, 'Now that we have spent £50 million on your learning what doesn't work, we are not about to throw that investment away.' It's a variant of 'Owe your bank £1,000 it's your problem, owe it a million and it's theirs.'

How did it go?

Q **I made a new contact with the managing director of one of our key customers, went to see her and she loved an idea I put forward. She wants me to follow it through but there simply aren't enough hours in the day to do my job and this project.**

A *Nice one. Unless leaving your current position for a while would be dangerous, what about a secondment from your company to hers for the duration of the project? This looks brilliant on your CV and you are cultivating two careers at the same time.*

Q **People have noticed that I am always in when my boss is. It's not good to get a reputation as someone who sucks up, is it?**

A *Tread a bit more subtly, squire. If you really are getting such a reputation it's probably more to do with how you talk to your boss and how heartily you laugh at his jokes than it is with always being there. A colleague of mine, Geoff, was a terrible crawler. Once he even came to a golf day, although he didn't play himself, and pulled his boss's golf trolley. At one hole the boss's ball went into the rough and his 'caddie' went streaking after it like a retriever. When he emerged from the woods there came a cry from nearby, 'What does it taste like, Geoff?'*

7

Culture club

If in an interview you get asked to describe your ideal organisational culture, just describe your ideal place to work and if you've analysed them correctly you'll be describing their culture as well.

You've got to be open and honest here. If the culture's not right, you'll eventually hate the job. You really are looking for compatibility.

Regardless of how well you fit the job and the job fits you, the thing that makes the organisation successful and you happy is the culture. It's the context within which everyone works. Use the interview to check that you understand the way they work and that you'll enjoy fitting into it.

THERE'S NO RIGHT ANSWER

Let's start with an easy one. If you're a very creative person don't go for a company that's very process driven and where strict attention to the rules and the small print

Here's an idea for you...

Think about times in your career when you've been very successful and enjoyed the job at the same time. Now think about the culture you were working in. What was it about the culture that contributed to those good feelings? Now try the opposite – when you were miserable. Comparing the two should help to uncover the environment in which you really like working.

is part of their function. Much of a lawyer's job is the careful interpretation of other people's writing. Maybe not right for someone who fancies herself as an innovator. So to prepare for this question define the elements of an organisation's culture that concern you. The list below gives you some cultural attributes to help you to do this:

Bureaucratic vs. meritocratic and open. On one end of this scale is the organisation that normally promotes through length of time in the job. You can't go from level 5 to staff level 6 without working there five years. You can't get to level 6 at all unless you're a graduate. The mark of a meritocracy is that high-fliers are put into challenging positions at the first opportunity. Openness tends to go with meritocratic. (The dining rooms are often a quick guide to all this: are they segregated by seniority or does everyone muck in at the same canteen?)

Internal vs. external focus. Do you want to work in an environment where your plans are pretty much dictated by the level above you, or do you want to drive your plans by thinking about what the external customer wants?

Quality/cost balance. Do you want to work in Rolls Royce, or do you want to work for a company that's increasing its efficiency so much that they can offer good products to a mass market?

Freedom vs. process and control. Are you a risk-taking maverick who likes to spot an opportunity, go for it and ask permission afterwards? If so, you're not going to be comfortable in an environment where any step out of line is met with tutting noises. Many people are more comfortable in an organisation that lets them know precisely where they are and what their sphere of operation and influence will be.

Fun vs. serious. What does it feel like when you walk in the door and talk to people? By 'fun' we don't mean frivolous, but some organisations take themselves less seriously than others.

Open vs. closed communication. Do they give a lot of information to a wide audience, or do they inform only those who need to know?

Team vs. individual. Does the organisation operate through its teams, or through its individuals?

Now mark on a scale of 1–10 how you think the organisation you're applying to works against your list of attributes. Also mark on a scale of 1–10 how the culture suits you. Where you can't answer the question through lack of knowledge, make a note to ask a question in that area at the interview.

> *'All my wife has ever taken from the Mediterranean – from that whole vast intuitive culture – are four bottles of Chianti to make into lamps.'*
> PETER SHAFFER, British dramatist

Defining idea…

IS WHAT THEY DO WHAT THEY SAY THEY DO?

Sometimes companies proclaim their culture as one thing and actually act in a completely opposite way. You can check on this in the interview: 'In your company accounts it says that everyone in the organisation is encouraged to be innovative. How does that work?' If they say that their customers drive everything they do, you could ask, 'What processes do you have in place to check on the changing requirements of your customers?'

WE CARE ABOUT OUR PEOPLE!!!!

This is a frequent 'Do what I say and not what I do' area. It's amazing how often the chairman's statement in the annual report contains something like, 'In the end our greatest assets are our people and I want to express my thanks to them for all their hard work' while somewhere else in the same report it's noted that the downsizing exercise has gone well.

Q   I made a huge assumption about the organisation I was trying to get into. They talked a great talk at all levels about being a 'collection of individuals' with a lot of freedom of action. That's how I like to work. I asked a few questions and it became clear that in reality they had a lot of rules, including, would you believe, firm rules about what you had to wear in the office and out at customers'. I almost wish I hadn't probed. What shall I do with their offer now?

How did it go?

A   *We're glad you probed and found out the reality. You're now in a good position to make an informed choice. It's much better to have found out now than when you've been working for them for a couple of weeks. It's a simple question: do the other terms, conditions and career opportunities make up for working in a less than ideal culture?*

Q   I found this Idea quite difficult. It's taught me that I've been pretty happy in most cultures even though I've been in some very different ones. How can I answer the question about culture now?

A   *Emphasise your flexibility and explain that you can work well and enjoy working life in different types of organisation.*

31

8

The seven deadly CV sins

Sometimes best practice is about the things we do; sometimes it's more about the things we don't do...

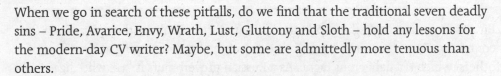

The biggest CV sin is probably to bore the pants off the reader, but there are plenty of other pitfalls awaiting the inattentive amongst us.

When we go in search of these pitfalls, do we find that the traditional seven deadly sins – Pride, Avarice, Envy, Wrath, Lust, Gluttony and Sloth – hold any lessons for the modern-day CV writer? Maybe, but some are admittedly more tenuous than others.

PRIDE

Pride can lead us to overstate our abilities. So, don't go describing your IT skills as 'excellent' when you know little more than how to turn on your PC. Equally, don't enclose a photo because you're damn good-looking, unless you're a model, actor or actress of course.

Here's an idea for you...

Avoid unnecessary repetition in your CV. Do not repeat things. Say them only once. Do not say them twice. Or three times. Once is enough. (Now can you see how irritating repetition is?)

AVARICE

Avarice can lead us to apply for jobs that are well beyond our capabilities. In truth, we're often more attracted to the salary than to the job itself.

The opposite of avarice is generosity. This means letting others have their fair share of praise. Don't therefore claim personal credit for a team achievement. Acknowledging the contributions of others from time to time will demonstrate that you can be a team player. On the other hand, don't 'we' all over your CV else you'll have the recruiter struggling to detect what you specifically bring to the party.

ENVY

Envy is about resenting the good others receive or the qualities they possess. In the context of CV writing, envy might come out in the form of sniping at the effort of others, which is a dangerous tactic. As a Russian proverb puts it, 'He who digs a hole for another may fall in it himself.'

Alternatively, we might feel tempted to claim experience and qualifications we don't possess in order to appear on an equal footing with others.

WRATH

Wrath is a furious level of anger that we'd like to vent on someone or something. If we've left or are leaving our current organisation on less than harmonious terms, maybe on the back of an acrimonious redundancy, there's a very human tendency to want to express those feelings. Just remember that your CV isn't the right place for this. It must remain a professional, dispassionate document – anything more emotive will do you more harm than good.

'Men are liars. We'll lie about lying if we have to. I'm an algebra liar. I figure two good lies make a positive.'
TIM ALLEN, US actor

Defining idea...

LUST

Lust is the self-destructive drive for pleasure out of proportion to its worth. Lust causes us to suspend rational judgement in the pursuit of gratification.

Remember that you're not obliged to accept the first job offer that comes your way. The offer may be flattering, but feel free to turn it down if it's a poor fit for the criteria you've set for your ideal job – salary level, degree of challenge in the role, location, future prospects and so on. On the other hand, when an offer meets most, but not all, of your criteria, you may choose to accept it or see if you can improve the offer through discussion.

'If you tell the truth you don't have to remember anything.'
MARK TWAIN

Defining idea...

'Some rise by sin, and some by virtue fall.'
WILLIAM SHAKESPEARE

GLUTTONY

An overindulgent CV gives too much detail and goes on for too many pages.

An opposite of gluttony is moderation. The perfect CV gives the reader the right amount of information. Not too little to prevent the reader from really understanding what you have to offer. Equally not so much information that the reader is swamped with unnecessary detail.

SLOTH

Sloth is about an inclination to be lazy and to put in little effort. With CV writing, there are two areas where lack of effort will undermine success. The first is where we simply take our old CV and bring it up to date rather than going for a radical overhaul and rewrite. The second is where we don't put enough effort into adapting our CV for each job we apply for.

Q **I recently read a book called *Sin to Win*. Are you telling me sinning is back in the doghouse?**

How did it go?

A *In this case, yes. This idea is simply intended to reinforce the point that sometimes best practice is about the things we should do and sometimes about the things we shouldn't.*

Q **Is this a definitive list of sins?**

A *Absolutely not, but it's a reminder that some things definitely don't work well in your CV. Talking of which, in August 2004 a recruitment firm called Marketing Professionals came up with its own list of the top ten CV sins, namely:*

- *Typos – around 50% of CVs contain spelling mistakes or grammatical errors.*

- *Work experience listed in wrong order – recruiters recommend you put the most recent position first.*

- *Unexplained gaps in dates between jobs – if you've taken time off, you should say why.*

- *Sloppy formatting – using inappropriate fonts, mixing up styles and sizes, failing to align paragraphs or bullet points, etc.*

37

■ *Trying to brighten things up with inappropriate use of colours, photographs, logos or fancy paper – this rarely puts you at the top of the pile.*

■ *Including irrelevant information such as holiday jobs or casual work.*

■ *Sending through a CV that has been constructed to apply for a different role – employers prefer a CV tailored to their vacancy.*

■ *A disorganised and hard-to-follow CV, with information scattered around the page.*

■ *Too much information – CVs should be kept to two or three pages and long paragraphs and sentences should be avoided.*

■ *Too little information – if it's too basic it won't interest the employer.*

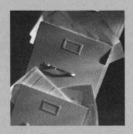

9

What am I letting myself in for?

The better you understand your target company, the more targeted you can make your CV. Which is why you'd be wise to find out as much as possible about your next potential employer.

If you uncover a potential corporate 'basket case', then I'd advise against joining them. If a company comes through your research with flying colours, however, then it should make an impressive addition to your CV.

Here are five ways to carry out the research required to separate the Enrons of this world from the pick of the bunch:

1. Phone a friend

Start putting the word around and you may track down somebody (or somebody who knows somebody) who either works for the company or is a customer or a supplier of theirs. These informal sources of information can be an invaluable guide to what's really going on inside the company.

Here's an idea for you... Ask yourself how good a potential employer is compared to where you're currently working. Remember that the company you go on to join will be the company that will take pride of place at the head of your CV the next time you make a move. How do you think that will play with future employers? Will they be impressed?

2. Google them

The amount of information to be found on the internet is quite staggering. In the pre-internet days, it could be quite difficult to research a company. Nowadays, to turn up at an interview without a detailed understanding of the company is almost unforgivable. You don't have to use Google of course. Personally, I'm quite fond of mooter.com.

3. The company website

Most companies of any kind of size will have one. Many of the best sites include an online copy of annual reports, information on company structures, copies of vision or mission statements, press releases and links to related sites. If you don't know the website address, it's always worth trying www.[name of company].com, .co.uk, .fr, .de... Failing that, a decent search engine should get you there pretty quickly. If there isn't a company website, that in itself carries a bit of a message.

4. Get hold of an annual report

You can often do this online via the company's website. There are also a number of ordering services you can use. In the UK, for example, it's worth using a service like the Financial Times' Annual Reports service, operated by WIL-Link (go to www.worldinvestorlink.com where you can ask for any number of reports to be sent to your address free of charge). Alternatively, phone the companies direct and ask them to send you a copy.

5. Track newspapers and journals

Scan the newspapers if you can, particularly the broadsheets and business journals like *The Economist*. If something is in the papers, chances are that the topic may well be high in the minds of people who work there.

'To be conscious that you are ignorant is a great step to knowledge.'
BENJAMIN DISRAELI

Defining idea...

You should be able to directly incorporate some of the information you uncover into your CV or covering letter. In fact, this should be a specific aim of yours, as there's real added value in letting the company know that you've put time and effort into finding out about them. And, of course, should you be invited to interview, you'll already have done a lot of the legwork to prepare yourself for that part of the selection process.

One final point. Leaving one job for another is a significant life decision. An informed decision is always likely to yield a better outcome than a leap into the dark. Before you think of resigning, are you confident that you know enough about the new role and the new company, such as its culture, the state of the balance sheet, and so on?

'I know all the tourist things. I know about the Queen, Buckingham Palace, driving on the left-hand side of the road and fish and chips.'
MALACHI DAVIS, American athlete, insisting he had the right credentials to represent Great Britain at the 2004 Olympics (and did)

Defining idea...

How did
it go?

Q   **I've uncovered one or two bits of information about a company I'm interested in that I'm not sure I like the look of. What do I do now?**

A   *This will depend on precisely what's concerning you. I'd suggest that you don't give even weight to every piece of information you dig up. If you've managed to have a chat with somebody working inside the company and you're happy that they have given you a balanced view, then that probably deserves a greater weighting than some newspaper sources. If you've popped the company name into Google and have come across a website that features a rant by an ex-employee, be more sanguine. By and large, I recommend giving the company the benefit of the doubt. After all, if you don't apply for a job on the back of your research, you may never find out whether that research was unfair. You can always withdraw your application at a later stage.*

Q   **I've come across a job I'd like to go for with a small start-up company, but unfortunately I'm really struggling to get any information at all about these people. How can I get the facts I need to make a decision?**

A   *It's a fact of business life that some companies will have no track record to speak of, but perhaps they have marketing material they can send you or maybe even a business plan. I'd be a bit surprised at the lack of a website, but you may have no choice but to get into conversation with them and then make your judgement in the light of what you been able to discover.*

10

Networking

There's more to networking than fishing out all the business cards you've accumulated over the years. Besides, exemplary networking is about quality of contacts not quantity.

Getting your network operating effectively is undoubtedly an essential component of the job-hunting process. In fact, outplacement consultants believe that as many as two-thirds of all job moves come about on the back of networking.

In one episode of *The Simpsons* Homer tries to get his boss (Mr Burns) to remember his name. Finally he resorts to writing 'I am Homer Simpson' on the wall of Mr Burns's office, at which point Mr Burns walks in, switches on the lights and says, 'Who the devil are you?' Perhaps not the most constructive way to register your existence with other people.

Networking has been defined as 'all the different ways in which people make, and are helped to make, connections with each other'. It sometimes gets a bad press from those who see it as a variation on the old boy network. However, as traditional formal hierarchies have died away and we become increasingly mobile in our careers, networking is more important than ever.

Here's an
idea for
you...

Concentrate on getting in touch with a handful of extremely well-connected people. Don't simply go through your contacts resolutely from A to Z. Ask yourself who your 'platinum' contacts are and establish when you're going to get in touch with them.

There are four main types of network:

- Personal (e.g. friends, relations, neighbours)
- Work (e.g. present and past bosses, colleagues, customers and suppliers)
- Professional (e.g. solicitors, accountants, bank managers, shop owners, doctors)
- Organisations (e.g. professional associations and clubs, chambers of commerce)

And here are six tips on how to build and maintain a set of contacts that will open doors:

1. Take the time and effort to build and nurture a network.
There's a book on networking by Harvey Mackay called *Dig Your Well Before You're Thirsty*, which makes the point that you can't make use of a network until you've put one in place, so it makes sense to be constantly developing your contacts.

2. Manage your network on an ongoing basis.
Having somebody's business card tucked away in your desk drawer doesn't necessarily mean that that person is a fully signed up member of your network. Here's the acid test: could you pick up the phone and call them right now without them struggling to remember you or taking umbrage? Let's put it another way: if you got a call from a fellow delegate on a course you went on ten years ago and you could barely remember them, how much help would you realistically want to be to them? As a broad rule of thumb, if you haven't had any contact with somebody for at least six months, it may be presumptuous to assume they're part of your network.

3. Be clear about what you're trying to achieve.

The more focused the message you feed into a network, the better the chance that something might come of it. 'I'm looking for a senior project management role in the pharmaceutical industry' is far more likely to register memorably and positively with people than 'I'm ready to move on. Not sure what I'm looking for to be honest. Fancy a bit of a change if truth be told, but beggars can't be choosers.'

4. Get your network on your side.

Don't antagonise your contacts by seeming to exploit your relationship with them. It's far more effective to ask people if you can tap into their advice and guidance than to look them in the eye and ask them outright for a job.

5. Make use of your network's network.

You can widen your network by using existing contacts to give you the names of other useful people.

6. Keep a record of who you contact and when.

When somebody gives you their business card, jot down on the back of the card where and when you met them.

Defining idea…

'There are four ways, and only four ways, in which we have contact with the world. We are evaluated and classified by these four contacts: what we do, how we look, what we say, and how we say it.'
DALE CARNEGIE

Defining idea…

'Eth: If Ron doesn't mix with better-class people, how's he going to get on in life? In this world, it's not what you know, it's who you know, isn't it Ron? Ron: Yes Eth, and I don't know either of them.'
FRANK MUIR and DENIS NORDEN, from BBC Radio's The Glums

How did it go?

Q   **I'd like to network more, but I only have a handful of useful contacts. How should I go about it?**

A   *The secret is not to take your network at face value. Could you diversify your contacts? For example, if you know just five people in each of those four main categories I mentioned (personal, work, professionals and organisations) and those five people can each connect you to five more people, that's one hundred people already.*

Q   **That all sounds very energy sapping. Isn't there an easier or less intensive way to network?**

A   *You have a point – to a degree. There are avid networkers I know who have three thousand people on their Christmas card list; for 95% of those people, that card is the only point of contact every year. I get cards every year from mystery well-wishers that I probably met at a function months or years ago. I can't imagine that it's at all productive for them. I know that it's damned annoying for me. If you don't have a passion for networking, leave the bulk buying of Christmas cards to others and concentrate on a few high-value contacts instead. They could be the president or chair of a particular society or group, or even somebody who has particular good contacts in a company you'd love to work for.*

11

On your bike?

Only one thing gets you down, and hence stressed, more than work. Not working.

For periods when you're 'resting', or times when you're not earning, you need this idea.

Paradoxically, one of the most stressed periods of any life is when you don't have to worry about the nine-to-five because for whatever reason you're no longer in paid employment.

People in low-paid, menial jobs are far more stressed than thrusting Type A folk. They have little control over their working life and there's nothing more stressful than lack of control. Those made redundant or who are 'between jobs', women who have had children and opted to stay at home – anyone basically who doesn't get paid (note, I didn't say who doesn't work) is vulnerable to the stress of the 'no work' phenomenon.

What's the answer?

Here's an idea for you...

Aim for excellence. You may be an adequate cook. Use your time 'off' to become a brilliant one. You may love reading. Become an exemplary reader. List all those classic novels, you've been meaning to read but never got round to.

TAKE CONTROL

If you're looking for a job, don't fritter away time worrying while making half-hearted or piecemeal attempts to find one. You need a strategy. You need short-term and long-term goals. You need to break these goals down into tasks and you need to schedule these tasks in your diary. You know this. It's just that when you're anxious it's a lot easier to spend hours fine-tuning your CV and waiting for the phone to ring than to be proactive.

Call every contact you know. Look into part-time or casual work that will at least give you some money until you get a job. At the end of the day having lists of tasks completed will give you a sense of achievement and help you feel in control. Enlist a friend if necessary. The hardest thing in the world is to call ten contacts and sell yourself to them, but asking a friend to call you at the end of the day to check that you've done it is a powerful motivator.

If you're a mother at home with children, structure is vital. Set yourself personal goals – just like you did at work. These goals should not just be about the children. Getting your jollies from 'achieving' with the kids instead of 'achieving' in the workplace is fine when they're really small, but your sense of displacement and low self-esteem may be greater when they grow up a bit even if you have no regrets about the time you've lavished on them.

BUILD CONFIDENCE

Here's a difficult tip but one that really works.
Ask five people that know you well to answer
these questions honestly

*'You take my life when you
do take the means whereby I
live.'*
WILLIAM SHAKESPEARE,
The Merchant of Venice

Defining
idea...

■ What is the first thing you think of when you think of me (immediately bin
anyone who says 'unemployed')?

■ What do you think is the most interesting thing about me?

■ What do you think has been my greatest accomplishment?

■ What do you value most about me?

■ What do you perceive to be my greatest strengths?

OK. A bit embarrassing. But just say you've been asked to answer these questions on
a job application and you're (becomingly modestly) stuck for ideas. What you'll be
amazed at is the different perceptions people have of you. It also helps you realise
that qualities you take for granted aren't qualities that everyone shares. You're
unique.

GET HAPPY

When you're short of money, isolated and bored, it's unlikely that you're getting the regular doses of endorphins that we need to stay happy campers. Understimulation leads to fatigue and depression. It's essential to manufacture highs and you have to do it daily. Make a 'joy list' of things that will give you a sense of achievement and happiness that don't cost a lot. By slotting them regularly into your day, you'll fire off endorphins and fool your body that you are still a high-flyer with endless cash to fritter away on life's inanities. You could decide to start every day with an alfresco breakfast, spend an afternoon watching a movie or have a glass of wine under the stars. Every day must have one pure pleasure.

Q   **I've been spending my between-jobs period looking for a new job in the morning and writing a film script in the afternoon. I'm being productive. Why am I so depressed?**

How did it go?

A   *It's very hard to keep the faith when you get no palpable payback. In my opinion – and it's only my opinion – it's worth including a few activities that have definite payoffs recognised as worthwhile by society. Doing charity work usually means others recognise you as a pretty good person. Working weekends as a minicab driver earns you cash. Less useful for this is writing your novel or launching your career as a portrait painter or looking after your children because society isn't good at recognising that these are worthwhile yet (although the last is changing slowly). These activities are not a waste of time but the fruit of your labour is purely subjective and in time doing them exclusively makes you feel isolated and defensive. Do the things you've always wanted to do by all means but also do some that will definitely result in rewards recognised by everyone.*

Q   **I've been looking for a job for a year. None I've been offered is paying enough money to make it worth my while switching off the TV. Why have I no interest?**

A   *You sound depressed. If your house is either a mess or anally tidy, I'm prepared to bet on it. Actually, the 'get happy' advice can work well for anyone with moderate depression if you give it a go but if you've only got enough willpower to flick the remote it might be just too much. All I can ask you is 'What's the alternative?' Without looking for help, nothing will change. Speak to your doctor, or seek out counselling.*

53

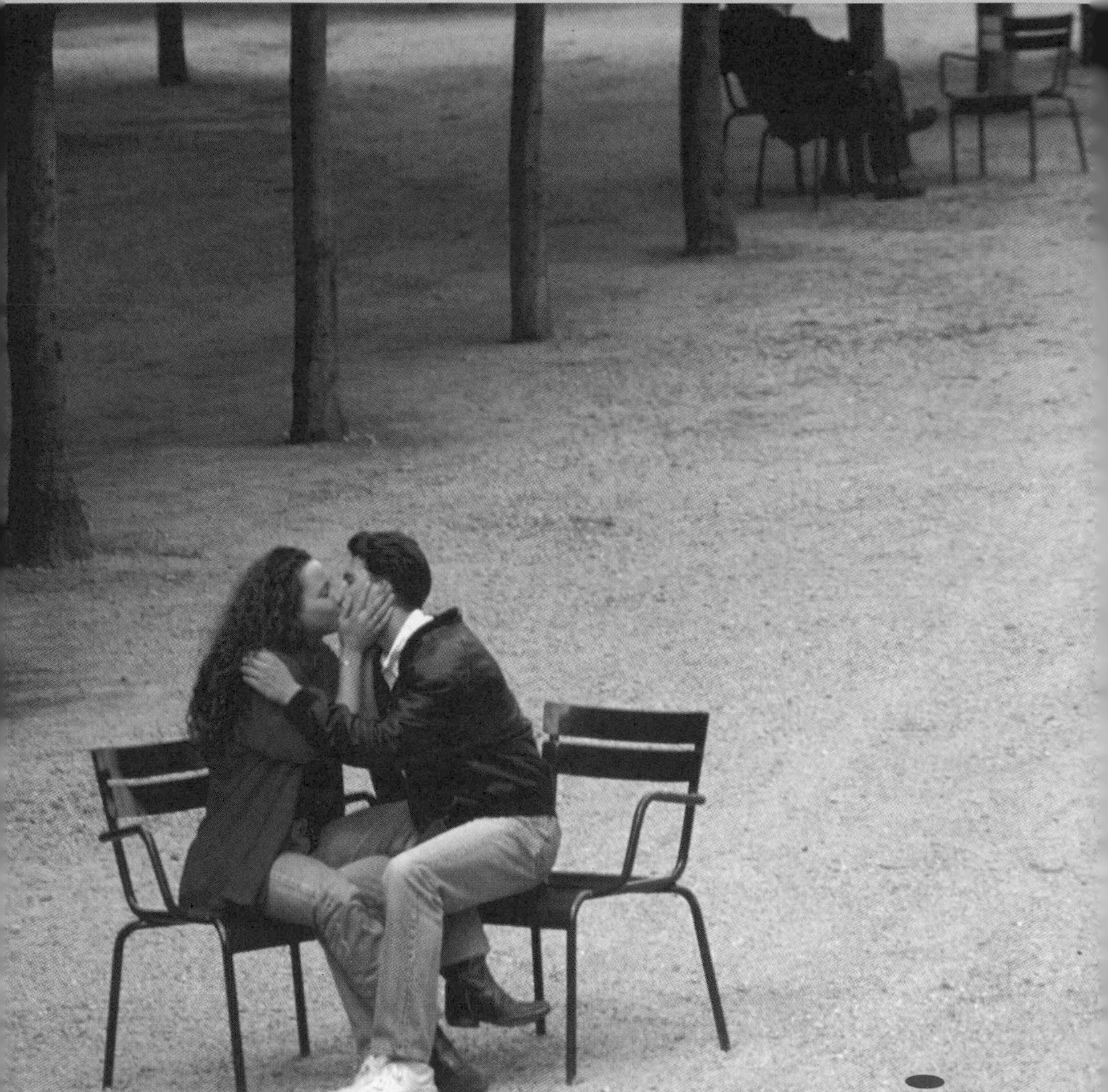

12

How do I persuade them?

We all want to steer people towards our way of thinking. So, what's the most effective way of influencing people?

When we want people to follow our lead, we usually try to find as many different ways to get our thoughts across as possible. If someone disagrees, we just try to come at it another way. However, does this actually work?

A PICTURE

Picture a pile of sand. If I pour a jug of water over the sand it's likely that some of it will be soaked up by the sand and that some of it will trickle down the edge of the pile making pathways as it goes. If I pour another jug of water on the same pile of sand, more may soak in and some may make new pathways. Most of it, however, is likely to travel down the original pathways and make these deeper. If I pour yet another jug of water over the sand it will be virtually impossible for the water to do anything other than go down the existing pathways, making them deeper than ever.

Here's an idea for you...

For the duration of your very next conversation try not to use the word 'I' – I think, I suggest, I don't agree. Concentrate entirely on 'you'. Ask 'you' questions. What do you think about this? How might you handle this? Let me test what you are saying to be sure that I've understood you correctly. That is a great idea that you have just had. This way you'll see how much more people are able to contribute. You'll also notice how difficult you'll find it to not take over and voice your ideas.

This is almost exactly how the brain works. When you give someone a problem to solve they'll begin to think it through and pathways or traces will be created through the brain. You tell them you think they've got it wrong and they need to think it through again. This they do and they may possibly find a new pathway but it's highly likely that they'll go down the same pathway, making that idea deeper or more firmly entrenched. Ask them to think it through again and it'll be almost impossible for them to come up with a new solution. It's not that they don't want to, it's just that the pathways have now been created and the brain finds it virtually impossible to move away from those pathways.

When you look at this picture it's obvious that continually trying to change someone's mind by telling them, yet again, why you think the way you do, is likely to be less than useless.

'I' VERSUS 'YOU'

When we run our Personal Leadership Programme one of the first things that we do is measure how well people communicate. We all have a perception of the way we communicate and most of us think that we're open to ideas, that we show caring to others and that we encourage others to come forward with their thoughts and suggestions. People are typically shocked and horrified by the results of the measurement. We absolutely do not communicate the way we think we do. I've as yet found almost no exception to this.

Without even realising it, we usually communicate by giving our point of view, giving our suggestions and telling people why we don't agree with their ideas. What we don't do is support their ideas, ask for their opinions, test our understanding of what they're saying, summarise all their points of view, or take their ideas and demonstrate their value by building on them. We don't invite them into the conversation. In the first way, all our focus is on 'I'; in the second, it's all on 'you'. The thing I've discovered is that those of us in what you might describe as the caring professions are frequently the worst! Why? I suspect because we feel that we really need to give people the benefit of our wisdom.

Actually, if you really want to influence people the knack is to ask questions that allow them the opportunity to think abut something in a different way. In other words, allow the brain to come from a different start point. First, focus on helping them explore their idea. Then focus on developing their idea to incorporate ours.

'To listen well is as powerful a means of communication and influence as to talk well.'
JOHN MARSHALL

Defining idea...

57

How did it go?

Q   **I tried the exercise you suggested and found it very difficult. 'I' was creeping in all over the place and yet I really believe that I encourage others. Is there any way to make this easier?**

A   *Unfortunately not. There are so many reasons why most of us end up communicating in this way and a lot of these appear to be good reasons. You now want to change lifetime habits. What I do suggest you do is ask the people closest to you – at home and work – to give you feedback on how you're coming across. Ask them to tell you honestly whether you're asking for their opinions, listening to them, supporting their ideas, and so on.*

Q   **I'm trying to do this and getting lots of strange looks from my team. This is almost putting me off to the point where I'm tempted to revert. How can I handle this?**

A   *If you suddenly change your behaviour it's not surprising that they may be confused. They may also mistrust what's going on. Under these circumstances I invariably give the same advice – label it! By that I mean explain what you're doing and why – because it makes sense to you and will help you become more effective as a leader. If you tell them that you need help in doing this they're almost certain to support you. Remember that you can't develop other leaders by telling them what to do all the time.*

13

You've done what?

Go-getters take risks and sometimes risks go wrong. When things go wrong people can get upset and angry. Sometimes doing the right thing for your career means that you have to deal with or even provoke someone's anger.

What happens when you stir up a hornets' nest? You might just find it works out in your favour.

An old trooper of a colleague of mine, John, had a problem client Alan. Alan never accepted that John and his company were doing the best job they could and giving a good service. He did what probably the worst of customers do – he kicked a willing horse. Alan was the training manager of a huge international company. The managing director of the company didn't see the need to meet the people who were training her staff, so John couldn't get round Alan and talk sense to her. John took this quietly for a while until he felt that the success of the client as well as the success of his company was threatened by this difficult, or ugly, person.

Here's an idea for you...

Never try to reason with an angry person. Never go back with any aggression towards an angry person. Apologise. If you feel you have nothing to apologise for then at least say you are sorry that the person is upset. Try to find something to be sympathetic about; perhaps by saying that, yes, they have every right to be angry and that you would be angry in their place. Offer to meet them again later, or if you are on the phone offer to go and see them. Don't try to look for a solution to the problem until the heat is out of the scene, perhaps not even that day.

PLANNING THE STRATEGY

Alan was a cold, clinical bully. He got his own way without raising his voice or losing his temper in any way. He was a frustrating man. 'Right,' thought John, 'what is the objective here?' He decided he had to get to the MD, impress her with some new ideas and start a new way of taking training forward with much less interference from Alan. A bold course was called for: he would deliberately make Alan angry. He reasoned that an angry Alan would get on the phone to Brian, John's boss, and complain very vociferously. Brian would write to Alan's MD suggesting that they had to meet to bring the relationship back into line. They would play it by ear from there.

CARRYING IT THROUGH

During their next telephone call John started to get angry with Alan; instead of holding back as usual he let rip and called Alan a lot of names including one of the few words rarely printed in full. He banged the phone down and strolled into Brian's office.

'I've just called Alan a c***.' 'You've done what?' gasped Brian, 'I've just called Alan a c***,' repeated John. 'But you shouldn't have done that.' 'I know I shouldn't have done it, but I have. So let's work out what we do about it.' 'But... but... but... you shouldn't have done that.' 'Yes, Brian I know that; so what do you suggest we do?' At that moment Brian's phone rang and the first part of the strategy had worked. On the line was an absolutely furious Alan.

Do you want to know the end of the John story? The strategy worked inasmuch as Brian got in to see the MD and a new relationship was formed. John, however, was not part of this new arrangement. Alan refused point blank to deal with him. Over a drink one night John confided to me that being pulled off the account was his plan B.

FINALLY

Ambitious people do not duck issues because they fear a person's anger; rather they learn to deal with it.

Defining idea...

'Anyone can become angry. That is easy. But to be angry with the right person, to the right degree, at the right time, for the right purpose and in the right way – that is not easy.'
ARISTOTLE

How did
it go?

Q **I remembered this idea this morning when I went in to the marketing department and found that my lot had completely ruined an expensive carpet by not covering it up while they repainted the false ceiling. I apologised whole-heartedly, and eventually a very angry manager calmed down. 'Right,' I said, 'Let's work out what we need to do to get this carpet as back to normal as we possibly can.' Then, guess what? She kicked off again, bringing up an array of incidents that I remembered from some time back when there had been other glitches in the maintenance service?**

A *Ah yes, sorry, I should have mentioned that. When people get angry and start to complain they rarely keep to a single point. They will rake up old faults, sometimes very old ones. You have to make sure they have got it all off their chest before reason gets a chance. Ask questions like, 'I think we should take this opportunity to look at the performance of the whole maintenance service we provide. Are there any other places where you feel we have fallen down?'*

14

Get to the point

When you're conveying information in writing or at a presentation, front-end load your communications with the key summarising point.

Wouldn't life be so much better if more people applied some discipline to their oral and written communications and got to the point more quickly?

Whether as readers or listeners, we rely on the writer or presenter to structure what they're telling us into a logical and readily graspable format. When that doesn't happen, we are left to our own interpretive devices – our minds – to try and create some kind of order out of the informational chaos.

This lack of clarity can be very effective as a device in a piece of fiction, where part of the pleasure in reading the book comes from our being able eventually to tie these threads together. In the same way, the essence of the vast majority of detective novels is that we don't get to find out that it was the vicar who strangled the postmistress until we near the end of the story.

As communicators, we normally work to a different informational agenda. Conveying our point with clarity and as quickly as possible is all that matters.

Here's an idea for you...

Take a selection of email, letters and reports you've received recently. Read them through and then jot down what you think the core message is in each case. As well as improving your summarising skills, it will help you to focus your thinking on the key messages in your own communications.

To that end, there are two key things we can do to get our message across effectively:

Give the reader the big summarising idea first; then present the supporting arguments/ information

Present the above in crystal-clear plain English

Let's take each in turn.

SUMMARY FIRST; THEN THE DETAILS

Have you ever received an email that bears a passing resemblance to the following?

Hi John,
I've just realised that Helena will need a lift home from her drama lesson on Thursday afternoon. Sally's away at a conference that day so she can't help. So can we cancel Thursday – sorry. I'm also struggling to put together the draft business plan in time for Thursday. I'm hoping to get Mike's input but can't get hold of him until the weekend at the earliest. I will finish writing the business plan on Monday all being well. How are you fixed on Tuesday next week to meet up as an alternative to Thursday.
Hope this makes sense.
Dave

You can just imagine the thoughts going straight and unedited from Dave's head on to the computer screen. As a business communication, it's not disastrous but it's not great. Compare it with this:

Hi John
I can't make Thursday, so can we reschedule our meeting to next Tuesday? Mike's not around until the weekend and rescheduling would give me a chance to get his input on the business plan and then produce a finished version for our meeting.
Let me know what you think.
Dave

OK, not a literary prize-winner, but a bit snappier I think you'll agree. The key difference is that the most important part of the message in conveyed in the first sentence, with the supporting information trimmed to the key relevant information.

PRESENT IN CRYSTAL-CLEAR PLAIN ENGLISH

In his 1946 essay *Politics and the English Language*, George Orwell came up with a set of six 'rules' for writing plainly and clearly. They hold up very well as a set of principles for anybody writing in the noughties:

'I love talking about nothing. It is the only thing I know anything about.'
OSCAR WILDE

Defining idea...

1. Never use a metaphor, simile, or other figure of speech which you are used to seeing in print.
2. Never us a long word where a short one will do.
3. If it is possible to cut a word out, always cut it out.
4. Never use the passive where you can use the active.
5. Never use a foreign phrase, a scientific word, or a jargon word if you can think of an everyday English equivalent.
6. Break any of these rules sooner than say anything outright barbarous.

The secret of success when it comes to being concise is quite simple: think before you write. Work out what your message is and then set about conveying it as clearly as possible. Alternatively, stick with the stream of consciousness approach if you prefer, but use what you write as your first draft from which to produce a more concise and coherent final version.

How did it go?

Q   I've been asked to write an article for the company newsletter. Any tips?

A   Yes. You'll need to adopt a slight variation on the structure we've talked about in this Idea. Journalists have long adhered to the following three-part approach: (1) start the article by telling the reader the conclusion ('After long debate, the G8 group agree a $50bn aid package for Africa'); (2) follow this up with the most important supporting information; and (3) end by giving the background. This style is known as the inverted pyramid and works well in newspapers and magazines because it enables readers to stop at any time and still get the most important parts of the article.

Q   They've now asked me to produce a version of the article for the company website. Now what do I have to think about?

A   On the Web, the inverted pyramid becomes even more important since we know from several studies that visitors often read only the top part of an article. Start with a short conclusion so that website visitors can get the gist of the page even if they don't read all of it.

15

Vocation, vocation

The smart ones amongst us recognise that our learning does not stop once our formal education finishes. But the type of learning changes from being primarily academic to becoming more vocational.

It seems these days that if you stop learning you die (certainly the converse is true). Indeed, this has been shown to be true amongst the elderly. Throughout our careers we have to constantly reinvent ourselves and learn and apply new skills.

The rise of the vocational qualification is a trend that reflects the need to maintain our currency, but this requires a different set of skills to the ones we may have used in the past.

I have taken many vocational exams in the past, and I fully suspect I shall take a few more over the next 10–15 years. From taking the professional exams which allowed me to become a chartered surveyor, following courses in IT to allow me to get

Here's an idea for you...

If you are following a vocational course and working at the same time, keep a logbook of examples of how you will be able to apply the skills you are learning to your job. This will help you in two ways. First, it will make what you are learning feel very real, and secondly, it will help you apply the skills you have learned more easily when you are back in the office.

involved with technology projects, gaining a professional qualification in project management and latterly in management consultancy, my reinvention never seems to stop. Tiring as it is, I have little choice, and increasingly, neither do you. Vocational exams differ quite a bit from the academic courses you will have taken in the past. The major departures are:

■ They are much narrower than academic ones. Whereas academic courses are designed to cover subjects broadly, the vocational course is designed to cover a narrow subject to a much greater depth of understanding. In some cases, they can be very narrow indeed.

■ Many vocational courses have a significant impact on your career progression because they lead to a professional qualification. For example, if you are an accountant it is likely that you will undertake some kind of study to become professionally qualified, and if you pass you will be able to do more interesting work and get paid more for doing it (surely the only objective in accountancy?). In some of the bigger firms you can be sacked if you fail your exams. How about that for exam stress?

■ Vocational courses are designed to make you more competent at a subject. As a result they are often practical and you will be expected to apply the skills directly after completing the course. I believe that academic courses are there to broaden your mind whilst vocational courses are there to deepen your competence and expertise.

'What we have to learn to do, we learn by doing.'
ARISTOTLE

Defining idea...

■ Whereas you tend to study for academic courses in your teens and early twenties, most vocational study is undertaken once you are in work, and hence in your twenties, thirties, forties...

■ Vocational courses tend to be shorter, often lasting only a few weeks, and so your study is concentrated over a much shorter time frame. If it ends in an exam, you will have less time to revise, so this means that your study skills have to be in tip-top condition.

So what are the skills you need to succeed in vocational study? First and foremost is the ability to listen, interpret and apply what you have learned to real-world situations; it's practicalities, not theories, that count in this kind of course. Secondly, you will need to be able to get to the point far more quickly in any exam because the subject matter is much narrower than what you might have been used to. The questions you will be set will be more direct and they will expect a direct answer. Thirdly, you will be expected to draw on your own experience to a much greater degree than in your early years of studying. And finally, the nature of the course will involve a lot more time thinking through particular problems and case studies, so there will be a need to interact a lot more, work in teams and apply what you have just learnt almost immediately. Vocational study is much less passive than academic courses.

71

How did it go?

Q   What sort of vocational courses should I take?

A   The best way to figure out what vocational course is right for you is to consider your career needs. If you have a long-term plan, assess your learning requirements against that. You might also want to place it into a broader lifelong learning agenda if you have one.

Q   And I do that how, precisely?

A   If your employer provides this kind of service then all the better, because they will have HR professionals to help you assess your career goals and will usually have courses that match your career trajectory. Of course, most employers don't have that kind of thing, so you'll have to think about the skills you want to develop and then pursue a course that is able to give you them. The best way to do this is to carry out a skills assessment.

Q   Do professional qualifications matter that much these days?

A   It all depends. I have a number of professional qualifications which I no longer need. They were important at the time because they opened doors. I feel that professional qualifications are important where you have to demonstrate a level of expertise that is otherwise difficult to show, or where regulation requires it. So if you want to be a lawyer, accountant or surveyor, you will probably need a professional qualification. In some instances they don't matter at all, but at least they make you look important.

16

Try working for a nineteenth-century mill owner

Some managers are just plain bastards. They are renowned for it and most people try to avoid them. Only work for them if the pay is better, or if it helps your brilliant career.

Some folk just can't do the interpersonal skills bit.

One of these people, a production director, was instructing a friend of mine to bulldoze his project through by making people co-operate. 'I don't care if you make yourself the most unpopular person in the company,' he declared. My friend, who had had enough, explained that that was impossible since the production director already held that position.

I survived one such boss who even gave me a thorough dressing down in front of her mother. Perhaps that demonstrated her problem. I mean if you have to show off in front of your mum when you are in your forties there's something wrong. I got promoted out of her team. I remember meeting my successor in the car park. He was looking crestfallen and I asked why. 'Her car is in the car park,' he said, 'so

Here's an idea for you...

When you work for someone like this you will frequently find yourself listening to people slagging them off. The easy thing to do is to throw in your lot with them and get it all off your chest. Your brilliant career, however, demands the opposite approach. Suggest that people misunderstand your boss and that he or she is a talented person with, deep down, a heart of gold. Senior managers will appreciate how you defend your boss, your peers will start to suspect that they might be missing something and everyone will respect your loyalty. Managers notice any disloyalty and will remember it if they ever come to thinking about inviting you to work for them.

she's not only mad, but she's in the office.' 'Remind her to take her medication,' I suggested helpfully. To this day I have wondered whether he did remind her, and also whether she actually took medication.

There are always opportunities where there are problems. If a manager has a reputation for being hard to work for and is generally unpopular, joining him or her may be exactly the right thing to do to. There are a number of possible outcomes:

If he or she is successful, then you can paint yourself as the person who calmed the troubled waters and made success possible.

If he or she is unsuccessful everyone will understand that it was not your fault, and you will be left in charge when they leave.

If the two of you fall apart, you may just be able to get some Brownie points for trying.

KEEPING THE PEACE

I once worked for a fiery project manager who
rode roughshod over anyone he believed was
endangering his project. He had a fine line in
abuse, and never held back from using it. I developed a good relationship with
him and managed to tone down a lot of the vitriol he flung around the company.
I also worked hard on my relationship with his boss's secretary, and she and I spoke
often about smoothing off the rough edges of his direct approach. Between us we
held the fort for about a year, until even we were powerless against a particularly
vicious attack on a manager who was supporting an idea that happened to be the
brainchild of the managing director. My man left, and I took his job on an
interim basis despite my being very junior for it. I also, modestly, accepted the
congratulations of his boss for having kept the man's talented contribution
going for so long.

*'To know all is not to forgive
all. It is to despise everyone.'*
QUENTIN CRISP

*Defining
idea...*

How did it go?

Q. **I've got a boss just like that. The trouble is that slowly but surely I am becoming tarred with the same brush. Will people become wary of me and treat me as though I were he?**

A. *One thing you may be doing, you must stop. It sounds as though people think that the rough stuff is coming from you as well as him. Preface all communications with words such as 'Bob has asked me to give you this message', or 'I think Bob wants it done this way.' It's a fine line between disassociating yourself from the bad ideas and hostile presentation of your boss (good), and being seen to be disloyal (bad).*

Q. **My boss is pretty universally hated. I'm using your idea about not being disloyal, but it's starting to wear thin. People are more challenging about him and I am starting to lose co-operation from some people because they don't want to do anything that might help him. Has it come to the point where I should just stab him firmly in the back and move on?**

A. *Hang on a minute. You must feel that he can help your career in some way or you would've done that ages ago. If that is the case, then you could try the really hard option and talk to him about it. Find some way of saying that he is losing the assistance of people who are essential to his performance as a manager or to his career. Human Resources might be able to help by suggesting some sort of interpersonal skills training.*

17

How important to you is your work/life balance?

The answer to this is important, as much to you as it is to them. Make sure you do know what that balance should be before you go in. Here's a way of working that out – plus some suggestions to make them love your answer.

There's no point in just being a safe pair of hands for the job. That just puts you up with the others. Add some flair and evidence to your answers and you'll stand out.

Everyone is going to say that they're indeed looking for a balance and that their partner/children/interests blah, blah, blah are important as well as their career. Here's a quick process that'll help you to know what you really want and at the same time give you an interesting way of answering the question.

WORK OUT YOUR STARTING POINT

There are 168 hours in the week, of which you spend 56 in bed. This leaves 112 for living in. Draw a three-by-three matrix of nine square boxes and write an activity

Here's an idea for you...

When you apply for a job with a new company try to get a friendly contact in the organisation. Question them about the culture of the organisation and its attitude to work/life balance. It's very valuable to have that information before you go in for an interview.

heading in each of them. The headings will include some of the following: friends, relationships, family, alone time, personal development, health, hobbies, leisure, creativity, work and any other areas of life that you enjoy or endure. If you need more squares just add them. Don't forget to add areas in which at the moment you do nothing but which you wish to get involved in.

Now list the number of hours in a typical week you spend in each of these areas, convert it to a percentage of 112 and write the percentage in the appropriate box.

That's your starting point. You may wish to check what you have written with your partner and a work colleague to make sure you're not indulging in wishful thinking. If the percentages are just what you want, well done; you just have to think through how to tell the interviewer this.

One person who did this exercise decided that he was spending too many hours watching television and too many hours working. The box that suffered from this was the one marked 'wife and family'. He resolved therefore to switch the TV off between Monday and Thursday. He told his boss he was only going to work late three evenings a week and that he was leaving each Wednesday and Friday at five o'clock. He started to take his wife out for dinner once a month and told his two sons that every other weekend they could have half a day of his time to do anything they wanted to do provided it didn't cost more than twenty dollars. He actually implemented a plan that was OK with his boss and delightful for his family.

> *'It is impossible to enjoy idling thoroughly unless one has plenty of work to do.'*
> JEROME K. JEROME, British essayist

Defining
idea...

PLAN THE SITUATION FOR THE FUTURE

Now look at the areas where you want to make adjustments. For every area whose percentage you increase you have to make a choice about which area you are going to reduce. Add in any activities that currently you don't do but have resolved to get started on. Now convert the percentages into hours and see if you believe you have a feasible plan.

That's the exercise. Now turn it into a brilliant answer to the question. It's probably a good idea to suggest you've gone through such a process. Tell them what the answer is. Watch their faces, though; some of them may be workaholics and think that's the only way for an ambitious person to be. Add a safety-first rider like, 'I think that when anyone starts a new job they probably have to work a lot of hours to get it under control; if necessary during that time I'll work all the hours God sends.' You can also point out that people who achieve a good work/life balance tend to be more effective at work. It's not just the hours you work; it's your attitude to getting things done.

How did it go?

Q   **I'm trying to change my work/life balance away from work. That's why I'm applying for this new job. I'd like to work fewer than forty hours per week – thirty-five if possible. Is this an acceptable reply?**

A   *It has to be really. If they don't know and appoint you, then either or both of you are going to be disappointed. Careful how you word it, though. You're trying to look like a person who makes a good contribution at work but has other important things to do, not a work-shy skiver.*

Q   **I'm trying to get a promotion in a company I already work for. The team I'm trying to join are in the habit of going for a drink after work most days. Quite honestly, I don't fancy that and would prefer to use that time in other ways. Should I tell them?**

A   *Ah, no. When you join you'll find it easy enough to join them from time to time without its becoming an uncomfortable habit. We would put this time firmly in the work part of the matrix, join them to keep up with the internal politics and slip out when it becomes idle chatter. But there's no need to explain all that in the interview.*

18

Detox your CV

Draw out any harmful content that might raise negative thoughts in the mind of the recruiter.

You don't get two chances to make a first impression. Usually a potential employer will only have your CV (plus maybe a covering letter) on which to base their impression of you.

It's therefore only natural for you to want your CV to look as good as it possibly can. And part of that is about only including information that will make a positive impact on the employer. The reverse side of that particular coin is to excise any information that is likely to impact on the employer negatively.

Here are a few things that your CV will be better off without:

STRIP OUT SURPLUS CONTENT

We've already established that CVs are one-to-one marketing documents. They're about accentuating the positive. Applying for a job isn't the time to strip yourself naked before the CV jury and reveal yourself warts and all. Employers might appreciate your searing honesty, but you'll be unlikely to land an interview.

Here's an idea for you...

Use spellcheck, but remember it won't catch every error. An unnerving example is that if you left the 'l' out of 'public relations', spellcheck will happily nod that through, but the PR Director with the vacancy might be less forgiving!

Sometimes knowing what to cut out of your CV is a matter of common sense, but sometimes it's a bit more of a judgement call.

In the common-sense category comes all the gratuitous information, i.e. information you've not been asked explicitly to provide that is likely to do your cause more harm than good if you include it. For example, an obsession with extreme sports might keep your stocks of adrenalin high, but it'll probably cause employers a frisson of concern. Likewise, mentioning the penalty points you have on your driving licence can only have a negative impact. Or listing your personal website if it happens to contain pictures of you mooning in Faliraki.

In the judgement call terrain, matters aren't quite so clear-cut. It's more about tone and nuance. Here's an example. Let's say that you're applying for a role that's 100% about dealing with customers face to face. Describing the face-to-face element of your current role ought therefore to get the recruiter's interest. If you devote, say, two bullet points out of four to this facet of your job, it will come over as a substantive part of what you do. However, if those two bullets are out of eight bullets, then you're beginning to dilute their impact by implying that you spend a lot of your time in non-customer-facing activity. Should you place the two bullets in the middle or towards the bottom of the eight, then that will diminish their effect further.

CLEAN UP SPELLING ERRORS

Employers have a nasty habit of assuming that anybody who makes a spelling mistake in their CV is likely to make mistakes on the job. At the very least, you're guilty of a lack of attention to detail.

'The key to any game is to use your strengths and hide your weaknesses.'
PAUL WESTPHAL, former basketball player

Defining idea...

The following bloopers were all taken from real CVs and covering letters:

- I am very detail-oreinted.
- Graduated in the top 66% of my class.
- Special skills: Thyping.
- Objection: To utilise my skills in sales.
- I am a rabid typist.
- Skills: Operated Pitney Bones machine.
- Strengths: Ability to meet deadlines while maintaining composer.
- Work Experience: Dealing with customers' conflicts that arouse.
- Typing Speed: 756 wpm.

DETOX YOUR QUIRKY INDIVIDUALITY

No photo, no wacky fonts, no coloured paper, no jokes, no eccentric hobbies, no exclamation marks, no personal pronouns, no 'Curriculum Vitae' at the top of each page, no volunteered salary details, no mention of political affiliation, no early schooling details and no unnecessary repetition of facts.

How did it go?

Q **I think I've stripped out all of the damaging content, but how can I be sure?**

A *In a world that's constantly changing it's hard to be certain that you've excised every last hint of damaging content, but a good starting point is to get someone else to read your CV specifically with an eye out for errors. However, be aware that they too might not spot errors like 'manger' in place of 'manager' because we're inclined to read what we think should be there rather than what actually is there.*

Q **I'm happy that I've fixed any typing errors, but what about detoxing the rest of the content?**

A *Have another read of your CV. Go through it line by line and ask yourself whether each bit of information is relevant to the role you've applied for, deleting anything that fails the test. Then ask yourself whether the information is presented in the right order, with the appropriate weight given to each point. Remember that the more important the information, the nearer to the top of the CV it should be. Any highly relevant information on page two of your CV probably deserves a promotion.*

19

Come back in the morning

Know when to put things on the back-burner, and how to let them simmer there rather than just grow cold or go mouldy.

You might very well claim to be a night-time person — an owl rather than a lark — but the fact is everyone works more effectively after a good night's sleep.

Fair enough, if it's getting late but you're motoring and 'in the zone', then stay up and feed off that feeling. Fair enough too if you have a deadline and simply must produce *something* for the next day. At some point, you may have to think tactically about what you can get away with, and burn a bit of night-oil thinking up good reasons why you're not going to deliver under the original terms of engagement. But never, ever bother bashing away at a problem late at night just for the sake of it, when you know in your heart of hearts you're not really solving anything. That really is a waste of time. And nobody will be impressed with your tired haggard expression unless the work itself has clearly been worth the effort.

Here's an idea for you...

If you have an imminent deadline, take your half-finished work to the meeting, admit your problems and ask for help in fixing them. Sometimes this makes everybody feel creative and valued. (Be careful how often you try and get away with this, by the way.) If your deadline is not so urgent, best leave it for several mornings (or months)!

In most cases, admitting defeat and coming back to something in the morning can really help not only to finally complete a piece of work in a good way – but also can ensure that you're in some kind of condition to really deliver at the critical moments.

According to Woody Allen, 'Eighty percent of success is showing up'. If you expend all your energy working fruitlessly through the night, you really aren't going to stand much chance of 'showing up' in the morning – either you'll be in bed fast asleep or you'll turn up at the office with your brain about as functional as a boiled pomegranate.

It really is true that you can see things differently in the morning light, especially if you're well rested and alert. Indeed, changes in light generally can throw a very different slant on your work. If you don't believe us, try working in different types of light, both artificial and natural. Experiment with a range of different light bulbs, perhaps. At different times of the day move to different rooms that have more or fewer windows, or face in a particular direction. Get up really early and sample the light at dawn (but don't stay up to do the same thing). Similarly, try working at dusk. (More accidents at work happen then than at any other time, by the way. You've been warned, so don't blame us.)

Sleep can also bring with it all kinds of strange dreams and thoughts that may come to your aid in the morning. It's amazing, too, how just by letting time pass a problem can go away (shame it doesn't work with toothache). For most creative people it's tempting to think that things only happen because of your presence and your input. But actually things happen without you too. Plants still grow, the world still spins and often what seemed so awful yesterday isn't so bad today. Crucially, you may also find that if you leave something in this way, somebody else will come along with the necessary input to fix things.

'Why is it I get my best ideas in the morning while I'm shaving?'
ALBERT EINSTEIN

Defining idea...

'One must also accept that one has uncreative moments. The more honestly one can accept that, the quicker these moments will pass. One must have the courage to call a halt, to feel empty and discouraged.'
ETTY HILLESUM

Defining idea...

How did it go?

Q   **I hate giving up on anything – even if it's past my bedtime.
Wouldn't I be better off finishing it in one go?**

A   *Abandoning something that isn't working right now can be emotionally
difficult if you haven't got something else to move on to. You may well feel
that you've failed yourself, or that you 'aren't really creative', or that all
this was a bad idea from the start – but don't. Walking away from
something actually gives it the chance to find its own way back to you.
Maybe its current form isn't the right one for now. Maybe it's currently a
painting, but will come back as a performance piece next year. Always store
what you've got – never trash it – and bring it out for inspection at some
later date. Bring it out, in fact, when you're stuck on something else and
are having that same crisis all over again. If you do this with enough ideas
and projects, you'll actually always have something to move on to – and
that way you'll never actually be giving up on anything.*

Q   **I find it hard to stop. There's always something left to do. Where
should I draw the line (and should I touch it up, once I've drawn
it)?**

A   *There's a sense in which no project is ever really finished, just abandoned.
If you're the kind of person who goes on working on something long after
everyone else would have abandoned it, maybe it's time to impose an
overtime ban. Force yourself to go home early, arrange to meet friends
when you would normally be working – or just take a holiday. Consider the
words of W. Somerset Maugham: 'Perfection has one grave defect: it is apt
to be dull.'*

20

Be successful whatever your gender

It's easier to get to the top if you are a man than a woman. Here are some women's thoughts about how to deal with discrimination.

The statistics are depressing if you are a woman. Look at the number of female MPs; look at the tiny number of women who make it to the boardroom and the number of female CEOs of blue-chip companies. You would never believe that there is more or less the same number of men and women in the world.

If you want to change this in general by politicking to remove barriers and discrimination against women, do it in your spare time. If you are a career woman, look at it as a personal challenge, not a male plot, even if it is. Your job is to get to the top not to make the world a better place.

Here's an idea for you...

Career women also agree on another hugely logical suggestion. They say that childcare problems are probably more stressful and difficult to manage than the jobs themselves. Why don't more employers set up first-class facilities for the children of employees? If a mother knows that her babies are being well looked after, that medical care is available at the workplace and that she will not be dragged off if, for any reason, a child is sent home from school that day, she is likely to perform her job better. Look at your organisation in this regard and see if it is not a good career step to put up a paper with this in mind. (Particularly if one of the senior recipients of this paper is a woman.)

To write this idea I have spoken to a number of successful women and condensed their wisdom.

BE ECONOMICAL WITH THE TRUTH

A TV programme not long ago carried this message: if you are a woman in your late twenties or thirties, you are likely to be discriminated against if you go for a promotion or for a new job. Managers are prejudiced against these women: if they have children they may have to take some time off to look after them; if they do not have children then they may take maternity leave in order to start a family. The discriminators are not only men, but also women who are themselves opting not to have children in their thirties.

This is surely an occasion for women to ignore the strictures of Robert Townsend never to con anyone, or this book's advice not to lie on your CV. Lie your head off. Leave the kids out of the equation. Perhaps you might hint at the fact that it just isn't to be, and that in the circumstances you are going to channel your energies into a career rather than a family. This is probably not very good, but you will be able to improve on it. Economy with the truth was the preferred tactic of many of the women I spoke to.

Women have given me other suggestions for what to do apart from lying your head off:

Put off becoming a parent until your 40s (you can always freeze your eggs).

Have children and get your partner to stay at home while you cultivate your career.

Smack down the people who defend the current situation. They tend to say that maternity leave and taking time off for the kids discriminates against shareholders by damaging the profits of the organisation. This can't be true, can it? For a start it seems more damaging to the shareholders to ignore the talents of half the managers in that age group. (Frankly, I know some male managers whose general incompetence would probably kill a baby left in their charge, so goodness knows what they are doing to their businesses.) And who are these shareholders? In the end most shareholders are people building pension funds or they are pensioners themselves. If there are more men building pension funds than women, then this is a result of this discrimination, and there are certainly more women pensioners than men. Pensioners live off the equities built up in their pension funds; therefore giving equal rights to women managers cannot damage the interests of shareholders. QED.

> **'Women who seek to be equal with men lack ambition.'**
> THOMAS LEARY, psychologist

Defining idea...

> **'It is not the glass ceiling that holds women back from rising high, it is the children hanging on to their hems.'**
> POLLY TOYNBEE, journalist

Defining idea...

How did it go?

Q **How can I lie about the fact that I've got kids? It's bound to come out when I have started in the new job and then what?**

A *Good point. What women said to me was that by the time they find out about the kids you will have proved yourself and they will need you to continue in the role. They also said that it is much easier to get away with discriminating against women by not offering them jobs or promotions, than it is to avoid charges of discrimination if they get rid of someone.*

Q **I'm a woman. I have an opportunity to move into a new part of my organisation that is very male-dominated. Do women find that sort of situation impossible?**

A *They told me that they had to work very hard to overcome prejudices at first, but that they won out big time in the end. If you join an outfit where women at the top are rare, an increasing number of men are scared that you will shout 'discrimination' and will positively do what they can to avoid it. And if there aren't any women around, who's going to be that one female representative on the board? Get in there quick, it could be you.*

21

Dream a little dream

High-impact CVs reflect precisely what you're looking to achieve from your career. So, before putting pen to paper, consider what you want from the work you do.

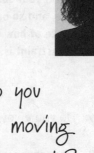

As a child, what did you want to be when you grew up? Moreover, how do you presently feel about your career? Is it moving along nicely? Going well but not well enough? Stalled?

Here are twelve questions that are designed to help you get a handle on the state of your career. Don't feel you have to answer each question in painstaking detail, simply go for those that seem the most relevant or intriguing:

1. In what elements of your career have you been most successful? And least successful?

2. What aspects of your career have you enjoyed the most? And the least?

3. More specifically, which has been the most satisfying role you have undertaken to date?

Here's an idea for you...

Make a list of the constraints affecting your career choices over the next few years. These may include financial issues, qualifications, where you live and work, your ability to relocate, and so on. Make a brief note of how important each constraint is.

4. With the benefit of twenty-twenty hindsight, are there any points in your career or life where you would have made a different choice or decision?

5. How do you feel when you get up to go to work in the morning?

6. What aspects of your current job do you enjoy the most? And the least?

7. Do you enjoy working with others?

8. How are you regarded by the people you work with?

9. Do subordinates, peers and senior managers hold different views about you? If so, what conclusions can you draw from this?

10. Have you had a new boss recently, say, in the last two years? If so, what impact has this had on the way you feel?

11. How ambitious are you these days?

12. What do you want out of the work you do? Are you getting it?

THE BIG THREE CAREER OPTIONS

Unless you're keen to retire, downshift, start your own business or continue as you are (in which case why are you reading this book?), here are your three main career options:

New role in the same organisation

Internal career development can be an excellent way of moving into new fields and learning new skills. Because this option involves staying in your current organisation, you wouldn't have the distraction of having to absorb a new culture or a different set of operating principles. You would also know who's who. If you're unhappy with your current work discipline, this can be a good way for you to find a more suitable area.

Similar role in a new organisation

This is perhaps the easiest proposition to take to the external job marketplace, as employers tend to be fairly conservative when assessing who they want to join their company. If they're looking for a Finance Director and you're already the Finance Director of a similar enterprise, you're much more likely to succeed than a Finance Manager from a completely different sector who's looking for a promotion.

'Optimism is a strategy for making a better future. Because unless you believe that the future can be better, it's unlikely you will step up and take responsibility for making it so. If you assume that there is no hope, you guarantee that there will be no hope.'
NOAM CHOMSKY, quoted in *Wired*

Defining idea...

Defining idea...

'*Ah, there's nothing more exciting than science. You get all the fun of sitting still, being quiet, writing down numbers, paying attention. Science has it all.*'
PRINCIPAL SEYMOUR SKINNER, from *The Simpsons*

New role in a new organisation

Hard on the heels of the easiest proposition to take to the external job marketplace is the hardest proposition. It *is* possible to change career direction and companies at the same time, but you'll need to work hard at it and be very convincing and persuasive about (a) why you're trying to make the move and (b) your ability to perform the new role effectively.

PAUSE FOR THOUGHT

Taking stock of your career is not a five-minute exercise. Neither is deciding what you want to do next. So, let's imagine we can hear a number of harp arpeggios with reverb to denote the passage of time...

ENLIGHTENMENT

I take it you've decided what you want to do next and you're going to need a CV? Excellent. So it's time for you to get started.

Q   **I've been examining my career, but I'm struggling with the self-examination. Why should I bother?**

How did it go?

A   *You're not alone. Most of us never get round to asking ourselves some fairly fundamental questions about the work we do and whether we've found our niche. Taking stock of our career to date is important, however, because it'll point to how content we currently are and whether we need to take some form of remedial action.*

Q   **I can cope with looking back over my career because at least there's something concrete to explore, but how can I get to grips with questions like 'What do you want out of the work you do? Are you getting it?'**

A   *To give some shape to your thinking, you may find it helpful to note what you want under the following ten headings:*

1. ***Money****: e.g. how much are you looking to earn?*

2. ***Working hours****: e.g. how many would you like to work? Nine to five or non-standard? How much holiday would you like?*

3. ***Job security****: e.g. how important is it to you?*

4. ***Level of challenge****: e.g. do you prefer to operate within a comfort zone or to be really stretched?*

5. **Type of work**: e.g. manual or knowledge-based?

6. **Independence**: e.g. working with other people or alone?

7. **Management responsibility**: do you welcome or hate it?

8. **Technical competence**: do you have or would you like a specialist skill?

9. **Work–life balance**: how important is it? Considering downshifting?

10. **Location**: e.g. indoors or outdoors? City or country? This country or abroad?

You should have a much better picture of your career aspirations once you've gathered your thoughts under these headings.

22

Please find attached...

A top-notch covering letter can be viewed as either essential or totally unnecessary and we've no way of knowing which is the case.

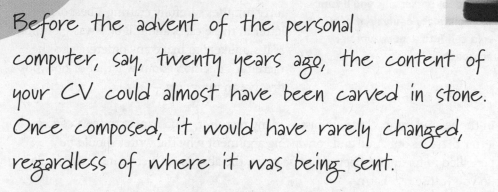

Before the advent of the personal computer, say, twenty years ago, the content of your CV could almost have been carved in stone. Once composed, it would have rarely changed, regardless of where it was being sent.

This was because much more emphasis used to be put on the covering letter, which was then *de rigueur*. Your CV would simply have described your career to date in fairly neutral terms. Your covering letter was supposed to map out why you were the perfect person to fill the vacancy.

So, in effect, the accompanying letter was the 'one-to-one marketing document' that the CV has now become. But because we now adapt and alter our CVs virtually every time we send them out to potential employers, a huge question mark hangs over the covering letter. In terms of how the covering letter is regarded nowadays, there are two distinct camps in the recruiters' world.

Here's an idea for you...

Always find a named person to write to. Anything addressed to 'The Personnel Manager' or opening with 'Dear Sir/Madam' is liable to end up on the desk of an admin underling. If, on the other hand, you write to an individual personally, you'll turn the epistolary equivalent of a cold call into a much warmer approach.

In one camp are those recruiters who bin accompanying letters on sight because they expect applicants to make their case entirely through their CV. They assume that people will produce a customised CV and that therefore an accompanying letter is simply a lingering nod to a piece of outmoded social etiquette. Spend forty minutes carefully crafting a bespoke letter in these cases and it'll be a waste of time as it's unlikely to make any difference to the recruiter's decision about whether or not you deserve an interview.

In the second camp, there are just as many recruiters who expect to see a covering letter that sets out a full and convincing argument why the writer should be pencilled in for an interview. In these cases, the absence of a covering letter would do your cause real harm.

The catch is that we rarely know which of these two camps we're likely to be dealing with when popping our details in the post. The safest bet for the prudent job-hunter is to therefore write a covering letter on the basis that it just might make a difference.

Your covering letter should obviously be typed, regardless of how neat your handwriting is. No recruiter I know will read a handwritten letter in preference to one that's typed. And regarding the content of a covering letter, the structure can be broken down into three sections:

'Everyone lives by selling something.'
ROBERT LOUIS STEVENSON

Defining idea...

1. Make the connection
Explain why you're writing at this particular time. If it's in response to an advertisement, identify where you saw the ad and when it appeared (this can help recruiters to identify which papers or magazines bring in the best response). If your approach is speculative, still try to give a compelling reason why you're interested in that particular company.

2. Make your pitch
Describe what you can offer the company. Try to make sure that every point you make is likely to be relevant to their needs.

3. Describe what's coming next
Take control of the process by saying what you want to happen next. Perhaps say something like, 'I'll call you in a week's time to see if there might be value in our meeting up' or a less pushy 'I look forward to hearing from you.' Follow up with a telephone call if you've heard nothing after ten days or so.

'To be persuasive, we must be believable. To be believable, we must be credible. To be credible, we must be truthful.'
HELLMUT WALTERS, German thinker

Defining idea...

101

How did it go?

Q **I've drafted a covering letter, but I'm not sure if it's any good. Any tips?**

A *If you've followed the three-point approach I've suggested I'm sure you'll have a good basic shape to your letter.*

Q **I'm quite comfortable with making the pitch and setting out what I want to happen next, but can you say a bit more about making the connection?**

A *You're right to focus on your opening gambit. A covering letter that reads like it might have been sent to dozens of other companies will get you nowhere. Instead, put some clear blue water between your approach and the thousands of cold CVs that turn up every day in corporate post rooms the length and breadth of the land. Here are three example openers:*

■ *'One of your colleagues, Gordon Ramsay in your catering division, suggested that I drop you a line.'*

■ *'I recently read in an article in* The World of Cheese *journal that you're planning to expand your operations into Europe and so I'm writing to see if you have any openings for...'*

■ *'I was playing golf with your MD, who suggested I got in touch.'*

23

Magnum opus

Creating a business plan is like baring your soul to the world because what is contained within the text will expose your aims, goals, aspirations and level of motivation for all to see.

Write the document for you, not others, and use it as the blueprint to success. Remember you're not writing a novel — less of the flowery prose and idealistic diatribe and more on the facts and figures.

A great business plan is really simple. No matter how complex your business, the end product should give any reader, no matter what their background, a huge insight into the business, your market, your goals and how you intend to succeed. A business plan should not be an excuse to confuse and wow readers with excessive use of management talk, industry lingo and overwhelming statements – it should outline your intentions in plain language. In terms of length, the business plan need only be as long as it takes to explain the proposition. Don't set yourself a page count and work towards that – write the plan, and if anything try and edit it down to 75% of the original size. A very long document will not help in raising funds, or

Here's an idea for you...

Before embarking on your business plan, obtain as many actual business plans as possible. Although there are no hard and fast rules about layout and style, as you begin to compare you will begin to see patterns. Use existing plans as a template.

encourage staff, or prove to be particularly useful in the future. In fact you will just bore people and maybe convince them that you are hiding insecurities about the business behind reams of stats, figures and a few poems thrown in for light relief.

Business plans really do reveal all, namely your own company's strengths and weaknesses, and are highly confidential documents that are not for public consumption. Be very careful who gets to see it and understand fully why a certain person needs to see it. Be sure to number each version and destroy older versions so that confusion does not arise.

A business plan is not a marketing document only comprising of forward-looking statements that will be nigh on impossible to achieve. A business plan is a working document, one that a good business refers back to again and again. It should lead your business to success and be followed, not locked in a filing cabinet once the seed capital has been secured.

What readers are looking for in a business plan is to be taken on a journey, from start to finish, of how you are going to make this business work. It's all very well concentrating on how many units you plan to sell and at what price, but don't lose sight of the fact that whatever industry you are planning to work in will have established competition. Acknowledge the competition and show categorically that you have researched the market. List your competitors' strengths and weaknesses. If you are able to obtain financial data (try the annual shareholder reports), quote this and show where your business fits into the market.

Defining idea...

When planning how you are going to tackle the marketing aspect of the business, don't just list what you intend to do, work out a timeline (for yourself more than for others) and give people a point of reference of when certain projects or campaigns will begin and how long they will last. Break down the costs for each individual campaign and explain the rationale behind the expenditure and timing.

When the plan is complete you will need to test it on someone you trust but who is not involved in the business or the same industry. Can it be read and understood by someone completely removed from the business? Whatever terminology or areas they find difficult to understand must be revised or explained – your plan must have universal appeal.

Once complete and fully edited it is time to make sure that the plan itself is well presented. Nobody is expecting gilt-edging, but having the document bound, or at least placed in a colour co-ordinated folder, will make you and your proposal all the more attractive – and the reader is also less likely to lose random pages, which helps too.

How did it go?

Q **None of the business plans I have seen mention manufacturing products. What use are these example plans to us?**

A *Actually you can find many US examples of manufacturing plans – and remember, every business is unique and therefore there will be areas you need to add that aren't contained in any business plan you have seen, and likewise there will be areas of the plans that you have seen that simply do not need to be included. Other companies' business plans should only be used as a guide.*

A **Is it better to lay out the business plan portrait or landscape?**

Q *I have written business plans in both formats and personally prefer landscape if I am including lots of financial tables. It really is just a question of preference.*

Q **I don't believe the market size and value estimates in the market surveys I am reading. I don't think they define the market in the same way as we do. How can I trust them?**

A *This is a common problem. It depends on the type of business you are in, but could you conduct some market research of your own? Sometimes this can be done inexpensively through sampling, and may still be statistically valid. You are right to resist the temptation to base your plan on numbers you don't trust.*

24

Find out what you are supposed to be doing

Your career depends on your organisation meeting its objectives, and your being widely seen as making a big contribution to those aims. Find out precisely what the organisation is trying to do before you work out your detailed plans.

Your career needs a winning plan of campaign that is on the same wavelength as your organisation's. Good careerists are better at planning than most people and they generally make sure they thoroughly understand their organisation's strategy before they craft their own.

The word 'strategy' is possibly the most ill-used piece of management speak in the business. Middle managers often complain that their board of directors doesn't have a strategy. This is normally not the case. The board's strategy may be wrong but it does have one. Maybe middle management has not been told about it or maybe they have misunderstood it. It is, in fact, a crucial function of the board to

Here's an idea for you...

OK, now we have agreed what a strategy is, get yourself a good definition of the strategy of any staff departments that are important to you. The marketing department is a good place to start – after all, they are responsible for agreeing the top-level strategy of what you are going to sell and to whom.

plan and implement a strategy, so you need a reputation as a strategic thinker to get to the top. Memo to self: Start working on that now.

Come down a few levels to team leaders and the accusation that they don't have a strategy can look truer. It is difficult for them to have an up-to-date strategy, particularly in organisations that do not give concrete guidelines on what a strategy is and how and when to review it. Difficulties abound:

- It is difficult for a team leader to build a strategy because it takes time.

- Short-term pressures stop the team getting on with the job of creating a strategy and even when it does, the strategy is frequently ignored whenever a customer or other significant pressure blows it off course.

- Your best strategy may be impossible because other parts of the business will not change to suit you.

- Building a team strategy needs consensus, so some team members are going to have to compromise – never easy.

But if it's difficult it must be an area where the ambitious manager can build some career points. Put simply, you need to build a strategy with your team, agree it with all your main stakeholders or interested parties, including your customers, and flaunt it. But you've got to know the organisation's strategy before you start.

KEEP IT STRATEGICALLY SIMPLE, STUPID

To work out your organisation's strategy it's useful to start with what it's not:

- The annual budgeting round. Don't mistake this for strategy. You come to the budgeting activities when the rest of the strategy is worked out.

- A large book of management-speak containing mission statements of 400 words that attempt to cover all the aspirations of the management team without pausing for breath. Here is one of these at board level...

'Our strategic intent is to strive for leadership in the most attractive global communications segments through speed in anticipating and fulfilling evolving customer needs, quality in products and processes, as well as openness with people and to new ideas and solutions. Based on our resources including technological know-how, market position and continuous building of competencies, we are well positioned to achieve our future goals.'

'Yes, but what are you going to *do*?' you long to scream.

'A strategy is no good unless people fundamentally believe in it.'
ROBERT HASS, businessman

Defining idea...

A mission statement like that always reminds me of the old limerick:

There was a young man from Milan,
Whose limericks never would scan,
When his friends asked him why,
He said with a sigh,
'It's because I always try to put as many words into the last line as I possibly can.'

Back to what a strategy is not:

■ A document produced by a staff function, carried around only by the same people, who use it solely to demonstrate that what the line departments are doing is against the strategy.

■ A matrix of numbers produced once a year and left on the shelf until such time as it is due for review.

Right, keep it simple, what is it? A strategy is a plan of what an organisation is going to sell to which markets and how. The strategic plan allows everyone to know how they should do their jobs, what the boundaries are and how the board will appraise any suggestions for doing new things. It is the strategy's job to bring focus to everyone's work. You must get to know it in terms that are not business school babble.

From now on when someone complains that the board does not have a strategy, confidently ask him or her to explain, 'What exactly do you mean by a strategy?' You will be amazed at the number who can't or who give you a line from a limerick.

Q   **I asked the marketing folk what the strategy is and, guess what, I couldn't make head or tail of their reply. It included words like 'paradigm' and more 'models' than a *Playboy* shoot. Who's got it wrong, them or me?**

How did it go?

A   *Ah, at a guess, them; but you probably asked the wrong question. Try three: 'What products or services do we sell?' 'To whom do we sell them?' 'How do we go about doing the selling?' If this doesn't work try a line manager with the same set of questions.*

Q   **How can I try the idea with a marketing man who says that the strategy is company confidential and that he couldn't tell me it?**

A   *This man is an imbecile or mad or both. Go and talk to someone sensible and shop him.*

Q   **OK I did it. Then, once I understood the organisation's strategy, I got the team together, and it became obvious that one area in our department is going to become much less important than it was. How do I pick up the morale of the people involved in that area of the business?**

A   *First of all, well done. The issue is out in the open and you can start to deal with it. Have you made absolutely sure that they are convinced that their jobs are going to become marginalized or even cease to exist? Can the people retrain for the area that is growing? If the answer to both these questions is no, then you've got a problem. The people are not going to try to change, and if they were to try you don't think they can make it. Is there some way you can generously offload this part of your operation to someone else?*

111

25

Be organised

Keeping a tidy desk and writing out long, neat to-do lists are all very well. But how can you be sure that you're going to end the day having really *done* something?

A big part of being creative is not simply about being 'inspired', it's about getting things done. So join the art and graft movement.

Since we all became 'knowledge workers' of one kind or another – and increasingly time-poor as a result – time management has become a whole industry in itself. The world is infested with time-management devices, theories and techniques to make them work. But don't be fooled by this. Above all, don't panic-buy the latest newfangled kit and associated manuals that will ultimately do you no good. We're here to tell you that at the core of all of this time-management mumbo-jumbo lies just one essential device: the good old-fashioned to-do list.

Whatever you use to create your to-do list – be it a piece of scrap paper, post-it notes, a white board or a PDA – the basic principles are the same. You need to concentrate on three things.

Here's an idea for you... **Write a list of impossible tasks. Put it away somewhere safe and only get it out at the end of a day if you're completely overwhelmed, or you feel you haven't really achieved what you set out to do. Looking at it might help you regain a sense of perspective and become re-energised for tomorrow.**

1. smart and realistic prioritisation of the tasks

2. the breaking down of big tasks into smaller, more achievable ones

3. the making of a new list for every new day.

When it comes to prioritising, remember Pareto's principle, or the '80/20 rule': 80% of all results come from 20% of all efforts. This means that roughly one in five of the items on your list are truly essential and you should concentrate on completing these. Everything else may be useful, but the world won't end if they don't get done.

Don't confine yourself to simple A, B, C-style rankings of importance, however: you also need to recognise that some tasks take longer than others. For example, one 'A' category phone call might take just five minutes while an equivalent writing task could take as much as five hours.

If you have one big important thing that needs to be done by the end of the day ('Send hard copy of manuscript to publisher'), be aware that a dozen smaller tasks are hidden within that one bald statement ('Check the printer works, check there is enough paper, print out the manuscript, proof-read, make revisions, print out fresh copy, bind/staple, write covering letter, buy large envelopes and stamps, check and write address, check time of the last post...and send!'). Each one of these smaller tasks needs to be itemised and allocated time. If you don't do this, how can you ever be sure that your one big to-do item of the day is really achievable?

'Failing to plan is a plan to fail.'
EFFIE JONES, author

Defining idea...

Sometimes, your list will become just too cluttered with tasks, big and small. To combat this, make two separate lists: one of things you *absolutely* need to do today and another of things you might get round to if you have the time or inclination. Don't even think about looking at the second list until the first has been dealt with.

The end of each working day is an important time. It's then that you should compile your lists for tomorrow. Don't wait until morning and find that the first task on your new to-do list is writing a to-do list. And don't just re-edit today's list – start afresh each time.

Quite often people use up the last half hour of their working day tidying up and 'clearing the decks' for the next day. Don't. It's much better to greet the new day with a messy desk and a clear head than the other way round.

How did
it go?

Q **I never seem to be able to close off a task or a project. Why is there always something more to do?**

A *Try every possible way of completing a task on your to-do list. When you come to each item on your list make sure you either deal with it there and then, get someone else to do it (some big corporations refer to this kind of delegation as 'push-back'), delete it altogether or, as a last resort only, put it off until later. Don't be tempted to put it off until you've tried all the other options.*

Q **I'm great at making lists, but they never seem to help get things done. Why not?**

A *Don't mistake list-making for doing. Too much time spent making or reviewing lists is a big time waster. Spend no more than half an hour at the end of each day planning for tomorrow.*

Q **Every task I set myself always seems to take twice as long as I thought it would. Why?**

A *Most things you succeed in doing will inevitably require follow-up and result in a new set of to-do tasks. When you have done something, always ask yourself: 'So what do I need to do next?' There might be things that you can safely defer until a later date, but don't let that stop you putting them on your next to-do list.*

26

What's your definition of the ideal relationship with your boss?

Whoever you're talking to, this one's important. You don't want to end up with a boss who you can't stand or, worse still, can't stand you. So you need to be open in answering this question.

Start from a very process-oriented view of the question. Then at the end talk personally.

The interface with your manager comes in three main areas: agreeing objectives and tasks, solving internal and external problems, and your personal and career development.

HOW DO YOU LIKE TO WORK WITH YOUR BOSS?

Start with agreeing objectives. Explain that you like a very thorough briefing on what they want you to achieve. 'I want to work for someone who is interested enough in the detail of what I do to ensure that I have a comprehensive knowledge of my project. I also like to know how my project fits into the whole divisional and

Here's an idea for you...

Although, when asked this question, it would be over-egging the pudding simply to describe the person you're talking to, it's not a bad idea to know enough about them to get a flavour of that into your answer. Try to research the actual person you'll be working for. Talk to one of their colleagues or preferably someone whose opinion you value who works for them. Plainly, this is more likely to happen in an internal promotion.

company strategy. I much prefer tightly written objectives that make it clear whether or not I'm on the way to achieving the right results. That I always think is the first key. I can then work on the rest of the details, only bringing my boss in when something is happening that's outside my control and is going to impact on my success.'

Now think about what else you want out of them in terms of problem solving. 'I like to be able to go to my boss with a problem whenever I judge the time is right. I also like it if they expect me to come with some analysis of the problem – I tend to list the strengths, weaknesses, opportunities and threats that arise from the situation. I also like to work for someone who encourages me to come up with my own recommendations for what we should do. That preparation work should make the manager's task easier. If you don't present the problem in that way, you're just alerting them that's something's going wrong and letting them work out what to do. I expect them to give me a fair amount of protection from company politics, and I certainly hope they'll keep making sure that what I'm doing is good for the whole organisation.'

Venture a little bit now towards the relationship between the two of you. 'It's very important to me that our relationship is very open and that we can say what we like to each other without causing hurt or animosity. We need to stay positive with each other: I find that then it just works, and the relationship develops well.'

HOW DO YOU LIKE TO GET FEEDBACK?

The quick answer to this is, 'All the time, and given in a way that allows me to exploit my strengths and work on my weaknesses.'

The longer answer looks at your career development: 'I want to work in an environment where my boss expects me to do well on the job I'm doing, but knows that I'm also looking to move on and make progress. I hope that they will recommend and send me on training courses that help me to develop as a professional with a good career.'

A summary would go like this: 'My ideal manager works in an open manner and with integrity. They make sure I understand what I have to do and fully support my endeavours.'

Watch out for questions that probe for negatives, like, 'Does your current boss do anything you dislike?' Straight bat needed here: 'Well, I'm not sure that "dislike" is the right word; but she tends not to give me enough feedback. I've shared this with her and it seems to be working better now.'

'To the ordinary working man, the sort you would meet in any pub on Saturday night, Socialism does not mean much more than better wages and shorter hours and nobody bossing you about.'
GEORGE ORWELL

Defining idea...

121

How did it go?

Q   **Personally I really like a boss to give me a lot of freedom and scope. During the interview with her it became clear that that is not her style. She seemed to want her people to play down a tightly controlled line. How should I have answered this question in these circumstances?**

A   *You could tell the truth and see what happens. She might not like it, in which case you won't get the job; but that may not be a bad thing. She may agree to modify her normal style if she really wants you, in which case she'll say something about that. If you really want the job, you may have to modify what you're looking for and keep your desire for freedom to yourself. Tell her that you can, if it's necessary, work within solid guidelines. You pays your money and takes your choice.*

Q   **During the meeting, I got no clear indication of the interviewer's management style. He played it very straight. I wanted to ask at the end of my answer to this question whether he fitted that description or not. Would that have been a good idea?**

A   *Yes, brilliant. Try, 'It would be good to understand how that fits with your style.' It's a nice tack because it helps to develop the two-way relationship.*

27

Show me the money

**How can you find out if you're underpaid or overpaid?
And what can you do about it?**

When you buy something for quite a bit less than you expected, you've got a bargain. When your employers pay you less than your market worth, they've got a bargain and the chances are you're being ripped off.

There's a great Tom Cruise film (and it's not often you can say that) called *Jerry Maguire* in which Cruise plays the eponymous sports agent whose job is to negotiate salaries and contracts on behalf of his clients (actually, client in this case – you'll have to watch the movie). One strand of the story follows an American footballer client of Maguire's who is very keen to realise his market worth and who is forever telling Cruise's character to 'Show me the money!'

So here's a question: are your employers showing you enough money?

123

Here's an idea for you... **If you follow any of the options set out in this Idea, just make sure you're comparing like with like. The salary packages that companies offer these days are sophisticated affairs. A particularly good pension scheme, perhaps coupled with other benefits and perks, might mean that the company offering the lower salary could be offering the better package. Try compiling a table of all the elements you'd like to see in your salary package – salary, share options, pension arrangements, car or car allowance, loans, special equipment like computers, etc. – and then use that as a basis for comparison.**

If you've only just joined a new company, then the chances are you've had an opportunity to negotiate with them and you've ended up getting the going market rate. If you've been with the company for donkey's years, then your salary should at least have risen to the company's maximum pay for your grade. That might not be your market rate – for example if you work in a lower-paying sector – but it probably won't be too bad a deal.

You may be at risk if you've been with a company for a reasonable but not a very long time. Have you been in your current job for 3–10 years? If so, you may find that you're being paid less than your more experienced work colleagues (not unreasonably perhaps). However, you may also find that recent starters are either being paid more than you or are at least snapping at your heels salary-wise.

Most employers have to pay at or close to the market rate to buy in new people. Rather fewer employers pay at or close to the prevailing market rate to retain good people. Once you're in the company pay system, your pay increases tend to be linked to the level of inflation and across-the-board company-wide pay deals. Not all company pay systems are fluid and flexible enough to recognise what is going on in your specific job sector.

If you are not convinced that you are being paid the rate for the job, it's worth researching your market value before your next salary review so that you can make the case for what you believe you deserve.

'We all strive to earn our self-concept level of income. If you believe you are a £20,000 per annum person, then you will always earn close to £20,000. People who earn a lot of money are not necessarily more clever or more highly qualified than people who earn very little money. People who earn a lot of money...have a higher self-concept level of income.'
RICHARD DOBBINS and BARRIE O. PETTMAN, *What Self-made Millionaires Really Think, Know and Do!*

Defining idea...

How did it go?

Q   **I've been trying to find what the going rate for my job is. Apart from scanning the job sections of the newspapers and professional journals, is there anything else I can do?**

A   *If you're wondering how to research your market value, consider talking first with your company's salaries department. Your employer researches salaries, and is likely to have access to many data sources that are difficult or impossible for individuals to come by. Some of the more progressive companies readily share this data with employees so as to foster an open dialogue about pay.*

Q   **And what if my employers aren't that co-operative?**

A   *If you are a member of a professional body, give them a call. They often hold salary comparison data.*

Another option is to start actively testing the market. Apply for a few jobs and see how you get on. If you can secure a job offer at notably more than your current rate of pay, you have a choice whether to move on or to use that offer to give you some negotiating leverage back at the ranch.

28

Get your own way with a consultant

External consultants present both an opportunity and a threat to your career. Exploit the opportunity and avoid the threat by planning how and when to get involved with them.

You need to know your way around the consultancy jungle: these guys could make or break you.

The Economist said it all in February 1998. An article entitled 'Management Consultancy: the new witch doctors' declared 'If you had to pick a single business or profession that typifies the frenetic second half of the 20th century, it might well be management consultancy. It has grown fast...it is easy to get into...it pays well...and, best of all, nobody can agree precisely what it is.'

Ah, how the mighty are fallen. Since the turn of the century the consultancy world has dealt with many problems – a dramatic fall in demand, scandals such as Enron and customers who feel that they were ripped off and deceived by consultants in the past. Daily rates, or *per diem* rates as the snotty big boys call them, have

Here's an idea for you...

Is there a tricky issue where you're finding it hard to get your own way? Could an outside consultant help? If so, make sure the case for bringing in a consultant is well made.

plummeted. At the same time many new consultants have set up shop. Many of these new freelancers were made redundant, especially from the large consultancies. They believe themselves to have many skills covering all aspects of business life. Few of them have many clients. Rude people call such executives who have gone out on their own as consultants the self-unemployed.

So the stage is set for the career person to cash in. Consultants cost less than they used to; so you can get flashier ones for the same price. They are hungry for work and they will tend to remember the people who hire them.

Arm yourself with the essential information:

- What is the purpose of hiring a consultant?

- What can an outside agency do that internal staff cannot?

- Can you justify the cost?

Now brief the consultant extremely carefully so that the answer they come up with is exactly what you first thought of.

USING A CONSULTANT FOR CAREER BENEFITS

As you know, one of the major issues that you have to deal with is company politics, the messy stuff that gets in the way of getting a job done. It is inevitable once you add the unpredictable element of people into any situation. You can use an outside consultancy firm to provide an unbiased view to the powers that be. The opinion may be more readily accepted than if it was something you'd come up with. And then there is always the added bonus that external advisers can take the blame for unpopular but necessary solutions to problems. Your reputation can stay intact.

Using consultants could be a really smart career move. Spend your company's money lavishly on them – everybody needs a pal and in any case consultants have to be kept in the style to which they've become accustomed. Such friendships then give rise to new opportunities in different organisations, because this is a two-way relationship. If a consultant has a client looking for a top person, and you've previously hired him into your current organisation at huge expense, they may very well introduce and recommend you. They need a pal too.

> '*Here's the rule for bargains: "Do other men for they would do you." That's the true business concept.*'
> CHARLES DICKENS, *Martin Chuzzlewit*

Defining idea...

How did it go?

Q **Right, I got a bloke in to look at an organisational problem I wanted to resolve. It meant some blood on the walls so I wanted cover and strength from an outsider. I hinted broadly at him that he should not go near my boss. So he went straight to my boss's boss on his first day. Why didn't you warn me this could happen?**

A *Sorry about that. It didn't strike me that anyone would believe any assurance from a consultant that they would not seek a higher level of contact. Career people like you would do it if you were in his position, so you should expect him to. It is much better to control their access than try to block them. Take them in to meet senior people when there is a purpose and, of course, assume that you are going in with them.*

Q **I was talking to a consultant hired by one of my clients. I believe they needed to talk to me in order to carry out their brief. They were very iffy with me and basically saw me to the door. How should I have got to make my point to them?**

A *Get yourself introduced by your client. If you blunder about with a consultant with as high or higher a level of contact, then you'll get into trouble. Get your client to write in the consultancy specification that they need to talk to you. Either that or get them to write a note to the consultant indicating why they should meet you.*

29

Actions speak louder than decisions

If you have taken a decision and informed your boss of what you and your team are going to do, for your career's sake make absolutely sure it happens.

If you haven't started the action plan, you may as well not have made a decision.

I've a friend who's an elderly painter and decorator. His children have moved on and he now has no dependants. He does not want to retire altogether but he does want to have more time for himself; but he's finding it difficult to cut down the amount of work he does. Unfortunately for him he is brilliant at his job and a very nice chap to boot. This means that his old clients all turn to him when they want work done and he finds it difficult to say no. Plus, his relatives and friends have been used to asking him over, giving him good food and drink and getting him to do some decorating.

Over coffee one day he asked me what I meant when I murmured that a decision is not a decision until there is commitment to the action plan and the first steps are taken. I asked him what he wanted to do in the spare time he was trying to create, and he rather coyly admitted that he had decided to take up golf. He then tried to

Here's an
idea for
you...

Pick a team member who has difficulty with the 'do it now' concept. He tends to agree to a decision made by you, himself or the team, and then finds loads of reasons why he can't implement it. Sit him down and tell him the story of the painter. Now get him to take a decision he has been prevaricating over and put the actions into his diary. Phone him just before and just after he should have started to implement the decision.

implement his decision. He resolved to take every Friday off to pursue this new hobby. Four weeks later he told me that he had not been able to do that once. I pressed him to commit to a lesson with the professional on the next Friday morning and another one that afternoon. We agreed that he would pay for the lessons in advance. This broke the deadlock and he started to play. He is now an addict and plays every Friday and quite often on other days as well – but it wasn't a decision until he'd gone into action.

Defining
idea...

'Men of action whose minds are too busy with the day's work to see beyond it. They are essential men, we cannot do without them, and yet we must not allow all our vision to be bound by the limitations of men of action.'
PEARL S. BUCK, American writer

NEVER DISAPPOINT THE POWERS THAT BE

Right, where is this stuff important? Most teams work with some operational targets that they need urgently to achieve. If your team is well organised you'll also have a strategic plan that includes a series of projects aimed at improving the environment in which you operate. If you implement these projects, life will become easier and performance will improve. Being career-minded you will, of course, have told your boss all about the changes the team is going to make – perhaps with a loud drum roll. But in the real world pressure is always on maintaining performance rather than developing new methods. In my experience a boss will ask three times how you are getting on with the new idea. The third time they hear your excuse that unfortunately there just has not been time to get it going, they will forget it and write you down as all mouth and no trousers.

'My choice in everything is to say nothing and go do it.'
LOU GERSTNER, American consultant and executive, CEO of IBM among others

Defining idea...

How did it go?

Q **Right, I got this bloke into my room and we discussed the fact that at our monthly team meetings he has never done any of the actions in the long-term plan. He could only agree and we put some very specific dates in his diary. He did them. Within a week or two major problems occurred on his patch. When I asked what had happened, he replied that he was following my instructions and so was busy with a new project as the storm gathered. That's why he had dropped the ball.**

A *You probably have a quite different problem here. If he deliberately turned his back knowing that issues would arise, he is sending a loud signal. Whatever he has said about the activities in the long-term plan, he does not believe that they are the right things to do or possibly that he has the skills and knowledge to do them. In other words he is not actually committed.*

Q **You're quite right about this.**

A *Thank you.*

Q **My team and I have so many half-started and half-finished bits and pieces lying around that they have lost interest in doing them at all, and I have lost credibility with my boss. How do I kick-start the important ones?**

Q *You've answered your own question. Go through the activities with the team, pick the important ones and throw all the others out. Sometimes when you are planning it is as vital to decide what not to do as it is to decide what to do.*

30

Eight potentially life-changing seconds

On average, it takes eight seconds to decide whether to continue reading a CV or to bin it. Here's how to capture and keep the reader's attention in those first vital moments.

At the risk of upsetting 'Fahrenheit 9/11' director Michael Moore, I'd like to propose that anybody about to write their CV should give a tip of their hat to Tony Blair and George Bush.

In recent times, prime ministers and presidents have placed great emphasis on the impact they can make during their first 100 days in office. It's a period of heightened interest for the media and the voters, and a good strong launch can create a positive impetus for the remainder of their term of office. The same principles apply when you're putting together your CV. So, how do you go about grabbing and holding the reader's attention in those first eight seconds?

Here's an idea for you...

Read your profile statement out loud to yourself. Is the language as natural as possible? There's a tendency for profile statements to be jam-packed with managerial gobbledegook and clichés. So, no 'proactive self-starter' nonsense if you please. That said, you do want to be upbeat and positive about yourself.

The fact is, if you can't convince the reader that you're well worth an interview by the time they're midway down page one of your CV, it's unlikely they'll read much further. Think of the first half of page one as your prime selling space. Your aim should be to try to feature all of your major arguments for being interviewed in that space.

Writing a CV isn't like writing a novel where you slowly tease and intrigue the reader, building gradually to a compelling climax. With a CV, your impact must be front-end loaded. There's no point in introducing a new and compelling piece of information halfway down the second page of your CV, as chances are the reader won't reach that point and so it won't be noticed.

So, what's the best information to put on that first half page? Well, virtually all recruiters expect to see your name and contact details at the top of the first page. Not just your name, address and home telephone number, by the way. You should also include your mobile number and an email address, as these are good indicators of your technological literacy.

Defining idea...

'When I've got say 50 or 60 CVs to look through, I simply don't have time to go through them all in detail.'
JOHN VILLIS, recruitment manager

After your contact details, I'd recommend including a two- or three-line profile statement. Think of this as a sixty- to eighty-word précis of what you have to offer that would make you a prime contender for the position you're going for.

'*Time is money.*'
BENJAMIN FRANKLIN

Defining idea...

By the time you've included contact details and a profile statement, you should still have around a half to two-thirds of that first half page still available to you. What follows the profile will vary according to what elements of your background and experience most closely match what the recruiter is looking for. If they're trying to recruit somebody who can do A, B and C, then you'll need to show explicit evidence of your attainments and experience at doing A, B and C. If this evidence can best be shown in your current/most recent role, then you'll probably want to go straight into your career history. If, on the other hand, you need to draw on your broader career and experience to prove your competence at A, B and C, a section called something like Key Achievements or Key Skills & Experience would suit your purpose better.

The recruiter is only likely to read on beyond this first portion of your CV if they're convinced you explicitly meet the specification they're recruiting against. This is therefore not the time for subtlety. Above all, don't rely on the recruiter to draw inferences from the information you provide. Concentrate on filling that first half page with as much relevant information as you can, paying particular attention to addressing the job and person requirements that the recruiter has stated. Given this, it goes without saying that to feature a piece of information that the recruiter is likely to regard as irrelevant is a definite no-no.

'*Time is precious, but truth is more precious than time.*'
BENJAMIN DISRAELI

Defining idea...

137

How did it go?

Q **Is eight seconds for real? I didn't realise recruiters were quite that lazy!**

A *Pretty much. Some studies suggest that the figure could be as low as three seconds, but no more than thirty seconds max on average. It's pragmatism as opposed to laziness in my view. Do the sums. A typical advertisement in the Sunday papers pulls in around 500 applications. Realistically, if there's one post to fill, then eight to ten interviewees should do the trick, with maybe half a dozen candidates in reserve. The recruiter's challenge is therefore to whittle the applications down from 500 to fifteen as quickly and fairly as possible. Allowing two minutes per CV would mean over two days spent going through them all. Besides, when they're in a position to eliminate 97% of the applicants, they can set high standards for making the shortlist. They can also afford to reject candidates for relatively minor reasons.*

Q **When companies are shortlisting on that basis, how can they be sure they're getting the best candidates?**

A *They can't. The process is designed to pick up those people who convey succinctly and explicitly how they meet the selection criteria. The candidate who might be the best in reality yet doesn't convey their proposition effectively is always in danger of missing out.*

31

How to love the job you've got

Sometimes you can't have the one you want. So you have to love the one you've got.

One in four of us wants to leave our jobs. We can't all do it at once, so here's how to cope until your personal Great Escape.

THE BOTTOM LINE

Hate your job? It's probably for three reasons – you hate the work (it's monotonous or stressful), you hate the environment, including your colleagues, or something else has happened in your life that makes work seem meaningless and you're ready for a lifestyle change. Or it could be that you're in denial. I'm going to come over a bit mystical here, because I firmly believe that sometimes we hate our job because we can't be bothered to address what's really stressing us out in our lives. Our energy is focused elsewhere and until we sort out whatever drama or sadness is soaking up our concentration, we're not likely to find the dream job anytime soon. So the advice here is not about refocusing your CV – there are plenty of other places where you can read up on that. But it will help you relieve stress in the short term

Boost work morale in a stressful workplace by starting group traditions beyond getting drunk on Friday night and moaning. Go out for a Chinese on pay day or book an awayday at a spa or have a whip-round every birthday and celebrate with champagne and cake.

and make you feel better about yourself in the long term. And that hopefully will help you raise your energy enough to eventually find another job.

LOVE YOUR SURROUNDINGS...

...Just as much as you can. If your workplace is grim and drear, you are not going to feel good. Clear your desk. Sort out clutter. Personalise your work space with objects of beauty and grace. Pin up photos of beautiful vistas you've visited or would like to visit. (It's a bit less personal than family pix.) But whatever you choose to put on your desk, change the visuals every couple of weeks, otherwise your brain stops registering them.

LOVE YOUR LUNCHBREAKS

A lunchbreak shouldn't be a scramble for bad food and a desultory walk round a shopping mall. Spend time planning. Every lunch hour should involve movement, fresh air, delicious healthy food and at least one work of art. Works of art are easily available for your perusal (art galleries, department stores) and easily transportable (books, CDs). Always, always take an hour to relax at lunch.

LOVE YOUR COLLEAGUES

Tough one. These could well be the reason you hate your job in the first place. If there are people who specifically annoy you, then find a way to deal with them.

Your local bookshop is full of manuals that will teach you how. Allow yourself no more than five minutes a day unloading your woes about work colleagues to a trusted friend or partner – not anyone you work with. This is not goody-goody – it's self-preservation. The more you unload your negativity all over the place, the more you are talking yourself into a hole of unhappiness and stress.

'People get disturbed not so much by events but by the view which they take of them.'
EPICTETUS

Defining idea...

LOVE YOURSELF

Turn up. Work hard. Do better. Lots of people who are unhappy with their work kid themselves that they are working really hard, when in fact their work is shoddy and second-rate. If you're not up to speed, improve your knowledge base and skills. If your work is lazy, look at everything you produce or every service you offer and ask yourself how you can make it special, imbue it with your uniqueness, breathe creativity and a little bit of love into it. Doing every task diligently and with positivity will vastly increase your self-esteem.

LOVE YOUR DREAMS

Most of us couldn't have got through school without the ability to drift away on a pleasant reverie of future plans. For five minutes in every hour allow yourself to dream. Read through job pages that aren't related to your present job. You may see a position or course that fires your imagination in a completely new direction.

How did
it go?

Q   I'm following your advice, so how come I'm still sad and low?

A   *Improve the quality of your life outside work. Build a social life you can look forward to, full of variety, stimulation and zing. Create a home you can't wait to get back to that truly nourishes and nurtures you. Learn something new, stretch your mind and imagination. And get out and meet people. The people you know are a very valuable resource. They inspire you. They introduce you to other people. They give you ideas. Don't specifically network but always be open to meeting new people and be the first one to chat to a new person introduced to your group. Find out what makes them tick. People who are open and kind to other people, respectful of others' ideas and competence, and interested in their lives, are exactly the sort of people who end up living their dream lives with their dream jobs. Don't tell me it's coincidence.*

Q   I do have dreams, but I won't be able to earn enough money if I follow them. How can I get over this hurdle?

A   *Write down all your fears about changing careers and then start writing ways you could save money or earn more. Energetic, focused people have opportunities thrown at them and I've never met one whom I thought of as being skint. Speed up the process somewhat by repeating out loud several times a day 'Wonderful opportunities and plenty of money are the rightful rewards for all my talent and brightness and hard work.'*

32

So, why do you want this job?

At an interview turn a question like this into a selling opportunity by using a double answer – balance what you'll get out of the job with what they'll get out of hiring you.

It should be reasonably easy to answer this question as long as you're going for the right job. If it's very difficult, then ask yourself if this is the right employer for you before you go in.

An employer wants people to join them with enthusiasm for the challenges they're about to face. Similarly you want to get into an environment where your working life gives you joy rather than grief. Research and good self-insight will give you the right answer to achieve both aims.

WHAT'S IN IT FOR ME?

It's probably best to start the dual answer with the straightforward answer to the question. It's another question that depends on your research. You've got to be able to reply in terms of the company's attributes as you find them. It doesn't really matter what the situation is; you can still paint it as ideal for you. 'Most people

Here's an idea for you...

This question really is one to prepare for carefully. The time will never be wasted, since this question will always crop up in one way or other. The best way to prepare is to find someone to role-play the interviewer and then try out with them the actual words you're going to use. If you can get someone in the same industry that would be best, but anyone with good experience of organisations or business should be able to help.

want to work for the market leader; I could use your name with pride' could equally be, 'I like the way you've made such progress in your industry over the last few years. A growing company like yours suits my energetic way of working. I really enjoy success.'

Now try to get in something about their reputation. 'I understand that you can offer me a stable, challenging and inspiring work environment – you certainly have that reputation. I think it's the sort of environment that brings out the best in me.'

Now compliment the company on what it actually does. 'Many people regard your products and services as the best around. It's a pride thing again; I like to work for someone who is passionate about service and quality. I think we share those values and that I would enjoy fitting into your team.'

AND WHAT'S IN IT FOR THEM?

Your unique selling proposition is you and your skills and experience. Try to work out a way of illustrating that everything you've done points at you being the right person for them. Perhaps start from specific experience. For a team leader in credit control: 'My experience in the credit control department of a builders' merchants was, frankly, a hard school. The building industry is always suffering from companies going under. I know about collection periods, credit ratings calculated from company reports and, of course, I've heard every excuse under the sun for not being quite ready to issue the cheque. I think that as team leader I would be able to help others to learn from that experience.'

Now relate the specific skills to the goals of the organisation. 'I understand the benefits to you of getting payment in on time or even before time because I've controlled cash flow for an organisation and seen the impact it can have on profitability.'

You can also be more open about your skills where you're sure they're appropriate. For a production manager: 'I've always scored well in problem solving and from what you've said you need to find some new ways of cutting down the waste at the end of the production line.'

Something more personal can emphasise your uniqueness. For a training deliverer: 'The fact that I've done a bit of amateur dramatics helps me to understand the "performance" side of running a training course.'

Now bring the three things together: 'So you see why I was excited when I saw your job ad; you seem to need a person with pretty much the experience, skills and interests that I've developed.'

'And so my fellow Americans: ask not what your country can do for you – ask what you can do for your country.'
JOHN F. KENNEDY

Defining idea...

145

How did it go?

Q   **I've thought long and hard about this. There's rather a good job in a company that's not doing very well. I think part of the problem is that their values don't include a focus on teamwork. They have a reputation for 'hire and fire' and come over as a bit 'every man for themselves.' When they ask this question should I point out that while I'm not sure I share their current values I think I can introduce some new ones that will help to improve their performance?**

A   *Possibly. Our first reaction to this was 'NO, wait until you've got the job and then sell the changes that you think they need to make.' But on second thoughts you could be right. Depends if you think that someone in the room is thinking the same way as you, in which case go for it. You could get the pleasant surprise of one of them telling you that they know they need to change in this area – in which case your preparation is ideal. (Sorry to be sceptical, but you should also bear in mind the words in script font at the top of this Idea.)*

Q   **I'd like to end this answer with a bold statement. Can I say that I would like to be in my boss's position within two years – in order to demonstrate my ambition?**

A   *Yes, but choose the words carefully. You're trying to make them feel confident about you, not insecure. Try, 'Finally, I have aspirations to get to your level in the not too distant future.'*

33

Well read

You need talent, artistry, political awareness and opportunism to enjoy the best your career can offer. You also need knowledge. This knowledge is much wider than your own industry. Here's how to get what you need to know.

Read external sources widely on and around your subject.

In trying to find out what makes great businesspeople tick, I asked a director of a large company what made his MD so successful. I had met the guy and knew him to be very clever and very quick. But what else was there to him? 'I'm not sure,' said the director, 'but I do know that he's in his office every evening until about 9.30.' 'What on earth is he doing?' I asked, 'Well, reading mainly. He keeps up to date with everything there is to read about the business climate, his industry and his customer's industry.'

Broaden your knowledge base. If you don't usually read a newspaper, get into the habit now. Try *The Economist* or *New Scientist* for a change. Perhaps a tabloid could give you some pointers on popular culture and what people are buying in droves.

Here's an idea for you...

Get a copy of your annual report and the annual report of your main competitor. Do some financial analysis of the two companies and see who is in the better state and why. If you cannot do this, go and see a friendly financial controller and ask them to help you, and give you some advice about how to improve your financial awareness.

INTERNAL ECONOMIC AND FINANCIAL KNOWLEDGE

Have you ever tried to argue with a finance director? They don't play fair. They have at their disposal an army of jargon, calculated, correctly worded, to wrong-foot any up and coming manager. When you are promoted into a new job, you have to make sure that you understand the financial implications of what you are required to do and what criteria you'll be judged by. Or would you rather compete with one hand tied behind your back?

It's a vicious circle. If you ignore the financial side of your job you'll start to lose control of the physical task. If you get behind with the administration it's only going to get worse. You must query figures that appear to be wrong, particularly cross charges coming in from other parts of the business or you could find yourself carrying a huge load of costs dumped on you by someone who has learnt their way around the system and has seen you coming. Even if there is no one in your organisation with such evil intent, you must not rely on internal costing systems, they are very difficult to get right and are notoriously inaccurate. The main difficulty is to make the systems keep up with changes in the organisation.

The point in the end, of course, concerns decision-making. You can make a decision that seems correct for the organisation but is financially wrong and vice versa. If you combine your functional skills with knowledge of the financial consequences of your decisions you are on your way to a great career.

'Looking back on my own career I think the one thing that perhaps helped me was the breadth of my reading about the oil industry and overall economic matters, in addition, of course, to being up to speed in the depth of knowledge to do the job of the moment.

SIR PETER WALTERS, Chairman, SmithKline Beecham

Defining idea...

How did it go?

Q   I went to see our financial controller and she referred me to an excellent book on finance (*Smart Things to Know about Business Finance*, by Ken Langdon and Alan Bonham, Capstone) and it brought me back up to speed. Trouble is, how do you maintain the knowledge when you don't have to use it very often?

A   *You have to use it often, I'm afraid. If you can't bear to read it every day, you should at least read the Financial Times every Saturday. It's a particularly good day to read it because it has a summary of events of the week as well as a good personal finance section that you'll find useful. Read particularly the company results pages. This tells you how companies are faring both financially and strategically. And when you've finished the FT, pick up the Wall Street Journal.*

Q   My financial controller seems to love problems. I only hear from him after something has got out of kilter. He then uses some obscure ratio to illustrate the point. I have to take his word for it and make the adjustments he wants. Is there anything I can do about it?

A   *Bastard. Have a frank exchange with him. Ask for his help. Creep around him until your nose is browner than a kid on the beach in Spain. You must get him on your side so that he will explain what he means and you can start to see the problems earlier.*

34

Liberate your thinking

Many people believe that there are barriers limiting their ability to succeed or achieve their maximum potential. These barriers need to be removed in order to allow a different and clearer way of thinking.

Limiting assumptions hinder our success. They are beliefs that we have about ourselves, others and our situation that limit our thinking and so inhibit our performance.

FREE YOUR MIND TO THINK

As a result of my mother leaving when I was a few months old and being sent away to boarding school at the age of seven, I carried around the belief that I had no value, that I wasn't good enough. If someone had helped me to remove that barrier, I could have expanded my horizons and thought in a hundred different ways. One powerful way to help someone overcome limiting assumptions is to ask an incisive question. For me a really useful question would have been, 'If you knew that you are good enough, what would you do right now?' Many possibilities would have sprung to mind. If I knew that I am good enough I could pursue a career that I

Here's an idea for you...

Think of an issue that's troubling you and figure out what's preventing you from resolving it. Now form the incisive question that will remove the barrier and allow you to think freely. To do this first take the words 'If you knew that...' and then turn the barrier into a positive and place it in the present tense. For example, 'If you knew that you can create the perfect relationship with your partner, how would you behave differently?' Ask the same type of question of someone you're trying to help at home or at work.

know I would be good at – public speaking. If I really knew that I am good enough I could start on the process of achieving my vision of owning my own company and owning the property I wanted for my children and myself to live in…and so on. Note that it isn't necessary to change my belief, but that this question allows me to think differently by jumping the invisible barrier in my mind.

This use of an incisive question can be an incredibly powerful tool in helping yourself or others to tackle new challenges and remove the problems that they believe are holding them back.

Here's a business example where a single incisive question opened a floodgate of possibilities to a chief executive who was my client. He asked me to dinner so that he could decide if he wanted me to become his personal coach. His major preoccupation in his division of a very large company was their difficulty in hiring and keeping the best people. That was to him the key problem in turning round the performance of the division. I asked him the question, 'Tell me, if you knew that you could turn this organisation into a preferred employer, one that's not just successful, but with a reputation such that people are desperate to come and work for you, what would you do differently from what you're doing now?' There was a ten-second pause and then he said, 'I really don't know.' I smiled and encouraged him to think further, 'I do really understand that but if you did know, how would you go about it?'

AND WORK OUT WHAT TO DO

The chief executive said that if he knew what to do, he'd start by sharing his vision with each of the division's 300 people, individually and in groups. After continuing for about twenty minutes he stopped suddenly and said, 'Where the hell did all that come from?' What had happened was that this man had been thinking about what needed to be done for so long that he assumed he didn't know the way forward, and pathways had formed in his brain so there seemed no way he could get fresh thoughts. All I'd done was remove that assumption by asking what he'd do if he did know the way forward. So, incisive questions are an excellent way to remove barriers or limiting assumptions so that we can think more freely.

'There are indisputable beauties in this world. The human mind is certainly one. An Incisive Question to free it is another.'
NANCY KLINE, personal development trainer

Defining idea...

How did it go?

Q **I believed that what was holding me back was the fact that I had to stay in the job I hate so that my family and I could continue to live in the manner we had become accustomed to. So I asked myself, 'If I knew that I have everything I need to find a job that I love and maintain our standard of living, what would I do?' And you're right, the ideas started flowing. But I can't expect my family to take the same attitude can I?**

A *Perhaps you need to sit down with them all and explain how you feel and what you're considering. Their concerns may well be a series of limiting assumptions. Try using incisive questions to help them clear these barriers so that they can think more freely about new possibilities.*

Q **Can I use this idea with my son who isn't doing very well at school and has started to think he's stupid?**

A *Definitely. See if you can get him to think about what he'd do if he knew that he is clever. So the incisive question might be, 'If you actually knew that you are extremely clever, how might you approach your work differently?*

35

Apply yourself

Always popular in the public and voluntary sectors, private companies are increasingly using application forms as a way of acquiring behavioural information about candidates.

For the job-hunter, application forms are a pain in the butt. You spend hours honing and refining your CV so that it makes your optimal business case for an interview only to find that your next potential employer isn't interested in seeing it.

However, from the point of view of many recruiters, advertisements that invite CVs these days are more likely to attract too many applications. In contrast, advertisements that ask for an application form to be completed typically have a lower response rate. So, from an organisation's perspective application forms can be a nifty way to reduce the time and money spent on the vacancy-filling process.

There's a shadow side to this, of course, namely that fewer applicants can mean a lower quality field. This means that if you can face the prospect of completing an application form without losing the will to live, you'll find that you'll typically be up against a smaller field of competition.

Here's an idea for you...

Complete the application form fully and don't skimp on the detail. And although it might be tempting simply to send your CV with the form, with 'See my CV' written in as many sections as possible, you'll come over as both lazy and disinterested.

Here are some reasons why organisations like application forms:

1. Application forms ask all candidates for the same information and are regarded by the Advisory, Conciliation and Arbitration Service *et al.* as good equal opportunities practice.

2. They allow the company to specify the information that applicants need to provide.

3. They allow a readier comparison between candidates because every candidate is completing the same form. Not literally the same form – that would be an administrative nightmare obviously!

TIPS ON COMPLETING APPLICATION FORMS

1. Unless you have the drafting skills of a Benedictine monk, it makes sense to take a photocopy of the form so that you can draft out a rough version first. Multiple crossings out and handwriting that becomes increasingly smaller as you desperately try to squeeze your doubtless brilliant prose into a tiny space on the form are great ways to demonstrate that you're as human as the rest of us, but they don't go down a bundle with the personnel department.

2. Use a black or dark blue pen – light turquoise ink may hint at your creative side, but it's a bugger to read and just as bad to photocopy.

3. Ask yourself what the recruiting organisation is looking for in the right candidate. Then tailor the information you provide accordingly.

4. Answer the questions as fully as possible, but don't waffle. Show that you can organise and express your thoughts clearly.

'Perseverance is a great element of success. If you only knock long enough and loud enough at the gate, you are sure to wake somebody.'
HENRY WADSWORTH LONGFELLOW

Defining idea...

5. There's normally a section of the application form that gives you an opportunity to make a personal statement. Use every last inch of it (and continue on a separate sheet if you need to). This might be your least favourite part of an application form, and it will almost certainly take the longest to complete, but it's a major opportunity to distinguish yourself from the competition. Highlight some relevant achievements and show that you've taken the time to find out something about the company ('Given your recently announced plans to launch a new product...').

6. Before popping the original in the post, remember to take a copy for yourself.

7. Knock up a short covering letter to go with the application form. Remember to quote the reference number and say where you saw the advert.

8. Go to the post office and splash out on some A4 envelopes so that the application turns up uncrumpled at the other end. Alternatively, liberate a few from the office stationery cupboard.

How did it go?

Q **I've just received an application pack for a job I fancy, but the blighters want me to fill in their application form. Can't I just send them my CV instead?**

A *You can, but don't expect an invitation to interview! Organisations that choose to use application forms as a basis for recruitment rather than CVs expect applicants to conform to their chosen approach. Barring exceptional circumstances, such as an incredibly low response, candidates who send a CV and don't complete the application form will be rejected.*

Q **But don't you find that filling out application forms is extremely time-consuming? I'd rather spend my days at the gym than filling out poxy paperwork.**

A *That's partly the point. Employers are savvy enough to know that using application forms will inhibit response rates. They figure that the people who can't be bothered to fill in their forms are unlikely to be the best recruitment catches. Let's face it, it doesn't say much for your motivation if an hour or two providing information to an employer's specification is beyond you.*

Q **I've decided to fill out the application form after all. There's not much space allocated to some parts and I'm finding it difficult to get over all the information I consider relevant. Is it OK to attach a copy of my CV in those circumstances?**

A *Check the paperwork from the organisation to see if they have a stance on CVs. Unless there's a note somewhere saying that CVs are expressly not wanted, go ahead. On your point about the size of some of the boxes on an application form, if you can't fit in all of the information you want to, continue on a separate sheet.*

36

Changing horses mid-career

If you make a move to a new company your fellow managers there have an advantage over you. They know the ropes and how to shine in the existing environment. It is therefore a very good idea to do something early on to question that environment and change it in a high-profile way.

When you are changing employer think long and hard about why they hired you.

If you are joining at a fairly high level it is likely that the people who hired you saw you as an agent of change, for a part of their business or culture which is underperforming – new blood, new brooms and all that. If this is the case, you can afford to take a few risks in the early days.

MAKE A SPLASH, WHY DON'T YOU?

Here's a brilliant example of making a great splash early on in a new outfit. A manager I know moved from one telecommunications company to another much larger and longer established one. He knew, from his competitive knowledge and from things said at the interview, that senior management were implementing a huge programme of change aimed at knocking the old-fashioned corners off those managers who had served with the organisation since the year dot.

Here's an idea for you...

Even if you are staying put in your organisation have a long, hard think about change. What in your company really needs to be changed? Think deeply and don't be held back by things that seem to be cast in stone – nothing is. Right, if the change is within your authority, just do it. If it's not in your authority, but it wouldn't be a suicidal risk, just do it anyway. If it's too much of a risk to take on yourself, go to the person who could do it and persuade them to let you do it. Try not to give them the whole idea or they might pinch it.

Many of these people were accustomed to a hierarchical, rather deferential culture where seniority counted highly. They were also struggling with the idea that the customer was king. On his very first day the new boy took action using the car park as his vehicle, if you'll pardon the pun. He removed every car parking space allocated on the basis of management seniority, and reallocated the best spaces to customers only. As he was doing this he realised that some areas were not only dark but also outside the range of the security cameras. So he allocated the next best spaces nearest to the entrance to those women who sometimes or regularly worked late.

At a stroke he got the support of those of his people who felt held back by the old guard, and of the more ambitious women willing to work long hours. His action also became high profile without his having to tell a soul – the old guard did it for him: they were fuming. They sent angry e-mails to the HR department and senior managers in all parts of the organisation complaining about this loss of their hard-earned privilege. They themselves gave him the oxygen of publicity. By the end of his very first day he had a very high profile. He had sorted the resisters to change from the enthusiasts for it, and impressed on senior management his grasp of what they were looking for in terms of cultural change. Senior management congratulated themselves, modestly of course, for hiring the right person for the job.

'Most ideas on management have been around for a very long time, and the skill of the manager consists in knowing them all and, rather as he might choose the appropriate golf club for a specific situation, choosing the particular ideas which are most appropriate for the position and time in which he finds himself.'
SIR JOHN HARVEY-JONES, former ICI chief

Defining idea...

163

How did
it go?

Q **I loved this idea and decided to have a go at a matter that has annoyed for many years – implementing IT. We have always felt forced to buy our IT services from the outsource company who took over our IT department some time ago. One of my managers has been saying that in one area particularly we could get a better service, and cheaper, if we did it ourselves. I told him to go ahead in a note that I copied to IT. Bloody hell, two days later I have the CEO's office on the line telling me not to do it. Can you imagine how I feel about the idea now?**

A *Still completely positive, if you ask me. This is brilliant. You are now in a position to go direct to the CEO to explain your idea. Get your bloke to write up the business case and send it to the CEO as your reply to their note. Sock it to them pal, there are few sweeter things in business life than getting the boffins in the IT department on the run. What a result! By the way, copying the original note to IT was asking for permission which is never as easy as asking for forgiveness. But in this case it has worked out just fine.*

Q **Why is car parking always such a sensitive issue?**

A *I'm not sure – but one hoary old MD advised me never to have enough car parking spaces because it gives everyone a focus for complaint. If you solve that one they might notice that they're also badly paid and working in other awful conditions.*

37

Back the right horse

You need to get noticed. Identify who is important to your progress, and get to them. Sometimes that will mean bypassing a human blockage – perhaps your own boss, or some obstructive gatekeeper who is there to keep you away from the decision maker. Here are some tactics to leap such hurdles.

Suppose, for example, that your job is to supply computer and telecommunications solutions to the finance department of your company.

Your customer and decision maker is the Finance Director, but on a day-to-day basis there will be a key person whom you meet regularly and with whom you form plans for future approval by the Finance Director. Such people can usually be divided into three categories – the Good, the Bad and the Ugly.

The Good are terrific to work with. They understand their business and they are happy to tell you all about it, so that you can come up with the best possible plan together. Cultivate such people. Latch on to their coat tails. Buy them lunch. Feign interest when they show you pictures of their family. Help them to enhance their reputations and they will help you enhance yours. They will probably be quite happy for you to talk to the ultimate decision maker should you need to, but they'll do it with you as part of the team.

Here's an idea for you...

Never ask Mr Bad for permission to go and see the decision maker. If he refuses (which he probably will), you're then in an impossible situation. If you go behind his back, then you're heading for a confrontation and the relationship will be ruined for good. No – do it first and beg forgiveness later.

The Bad are often bad because they are scared. They're scared of their boss, they're scared of making mistakes and they're probably scared of a brilliant careerist like you. They probably don't know enough about their business to really brief you on what it is they want and will probably bar you from seeing the decision maker until you have earned their trust. That is the vital element of dealing with the Bad – you have to gain their trust.

It should be quite easy for a cool careerist like you to do this. Achieve some good, high-profile results that end up on the Finance Director's desk, and make sure Mr Bad gets all the credit. But do this genuinely. If you have to, you can dump on him later by showing that it has been you and your team all along that got the results, but life is easier if you can avoid having to do this.

At the point when he trusts you, Mr Bad should let you meet his boss. There is a problem if he won't. Access to his Director is vital if you are to carry out your role. So, like it or not, you have to get to them.

Remember, 'it is much easier to ask for forgiveness than to ask for permission.' Once you have created a relationship with his boss, Mr Bad will never be in such a strong position again to get in your way.

Now for Mr Ugly. Mr Ugly is mean. He doesn't trust you, he doesn't trust his boss, he doesn't trust anyone. Quite often such people are bullies. You can't really play along with them if they are not allowing you to do the best you can for your customer; so you have to grasp the nettle and probably cause a major stink. Funnily enough, the way to deal with them is to cause them some fear, uncertainty and doubt.

'*It is better to be beautiful than to be good. But...it is better to be good than to be ugly.*'
OSCAR WILDE

Defining idea...

DEALING WITH MR UGLY

One of my salespeople had a Mr Ugly to contend with. I had to go in to see him and explain very logically that if my salesperson could not see the boss I would have to go in myself. I then displayed knowledge of what this bloke's competitors were doing and showed him that he was losing ground by not investing enough with us. I kept him just short of blowing his top and his uncertainty made him a bit easier to deal with. Unfortunately, however, he would not keep up with technological change and buy a 2960 B from us.

He would not even talk about it. The time had come to take a big risk. We made an appointment to go and see the Director, his boss, and we specifically asked that the meeting be with him on his own. As we had hoped, the director knew there was something wrong in that part of his business and agreed, albeit with at least a show of reluctance. We were pretty nervous; this was a major knifing job on a fairly senior person in a big customer. The Director's opening was, 'Now just before we get to the intriguing question of why you wanted to see me without Rob, I thought I better let you know that he has just recommended that we buy a 2960 B.'

How did
it go?

Q. **I have a product manager who, by your definition, is ugly. She has told me that she will arrange for my career to end if I so much as think about going to see her boss. There are some circumstances where you simply can't ignore a threat like this aren't there?**

A.   *No.*

Q. **Any ways of doing it apart from taking a huge risk of aggressive retaliation?**

A.   *Probably. The best way might be to come down the way to the decision maker. Work out how you can get the decision maker's boss to tell them to meet you. That way when Ms Ugly gets to know, you can just say that you were actually invited in to meet her boss. Alternatively, can you get to her boss at a social event or a conference or something like that?*

Q. **I don't like it – this woman is evil.**

A.   *Ah, come on. Nobody said having a cool career was easy.*

38

Take a test drive

Despite the fact that you haven't sat a test since you were at school, there's no need to feel concerned. You need to understand a bit about the tests and limber up your brain.

Bear in mind that the test is only one part of the process. But it's still a good idea to give it your best shot.

There is an intrinsic fallibility in making decisions based on interviews. The rapport that does or doesn't exist between interviewer and interviewee can lead to the wrong conclusion. This is particularly so if the interviewer is poor at the job. That's basically why recruiters use tests.

JUST WHO ARE YOU?

One type of test is the personality test. The good news about these tests is that there are no right or wrong answers and they're rarely done against the clock. The recruiter is generally looking for some further evidence of whether or not you will fit the role and the company and, of course, whether it will fit you.

Here's an idea for you...

Have a look at one or two of the big test companies. (Google 'personality tests' will give you a good few to choose from.) The site of SHL, a big player in this area, has a lot of useful information under the title 'Candidate Helpline'. Well worth having a look at the day before the test.

The only thing to do here is to be honest. Answer the questions as accurately as you can and you'll probably enjoy it. (Women's magazine editors are well aware of our partiality to ticking boxes if it's going to tell us something about ourselves.) Don't try to make out you're different from who you are. If you do, you'll be caught out in one of three ways: the test will pick it up, the test results won't fit with the data on you from the interview or you'll be offered the job on false pretences and will be found out when you're in the role. Be proud of who you are and represent yourself in a straightforward way. Anyway, if you try to second-guess what they're looking for, you'll probably get it wrong and do both sides no good.

Your answers will typically be looked at against a norm table of hundreds of people who have done the same test and a 'profile' will emerge which shows how you compare with the 'norm'. There is no right or wrong profile per se. The company will seek to establish whether your profile matches what they need for a particular role now and in the future. Typically, it will explore areas like your sociability, ability to manage in a stressful situation, degree of inventiveness, and attitude to working in a team.

HOW ARE YOU ON ROCKET SCIENCE?

The other type of test is an ability test. Although psychologists would deny it, ability tests measure some aspects of your intelligence. Again, your responses will be compared with a norm group so the company can see if you work with facts, figures and data more effectively than x% of the population. It's important to get the accuracy/speed balance correct, since most of these tests are timed. Try not to sacrifice accuracy for speed. Most testers would prefer to see ten correct answers out of eleven rather than ten right out of twenty. However, don't take too long about it. If you only answer ten out of twenty you can't get more than 50%. As usual, forewarned is forearmed. Find out from the HR people whether they're going to ask you to do a test and if so which one. They probably won't answer the second question, but it's worth a pop.

Other ability tests look at your creativity or dexterity, among many other topics. There's nothing you can do about these tests except refuse to do them and not get the job. Take a few deep breaths, keep calm and concentrate hard. Sorry to be like teacher here, but do read the questions ever so carefully. If you're going to be wrong, be wrong because you don't know, not because you read the question too quickly.

You've done the company a service by sitting the test; they must do you the courtesy of giving you feedback. If they don't offer it ask for it, politely but firmly. It can be invaluable feedback for your future. This is crucial if you sit the tests before the interview. You do rather have one arm tied behind your back if you don't get feedback from the test.

> '*When you do Shakespeare they think you must be intelligent because they think you understand what you're saying.*'
> HELEN MIRREN, British actress

Defining idea...

How did it go?

Q **You say that the test is only one part of the process; but I know for a fact that because of a test I was turned down for a promotion. Isn't this a real danger?**

A *Fair point. It's true that if other things are equal the test could tip the balance. It's probably quite rare that this occurs, but it may have done in your case. Ah well, nobody said life was fair.*

Q **I asked for feedback and they just said that it wasn't company policy to give any, and that was that. What else could I do?**

A *Try not to leave it like that. If you haven't succeeded face to face, send them a letter explaining the importance of the test results to you for your future. Maybe write the note to a senior person. After all, they can change company policy.*

Q **I've found out what the test is and I've done it before. Should I own up because I know what they're looking for?**

A *Not if you want to get the job, mate!*

39

Friend and enemy

When you start up your own company it might be your leadership and direction that drives the business initially, but it will be your staff members who are responsible for realising the dream.

Staffing your business with all of your mates from the pub will make you very popular, but unless you are planning to run a pub, it really is a bad move.

Hire the right person for the job and it can only mean success; get it wrong and it could collapse the business. Naturally, the first people you will turn to in your hour of need are your friends and family. You will no doubt be aware of their present circumstances, salary and job satisfaction – which is an awful lot of information and allows you to offer an alternative package and working conditions to win them over.

Employing friends and family can be the best move you and your business can make. You already know about their reliability, timekeeping and sickness record and there is a good chance that you will get more for your money in terms of number of hours worked and quality of work. On the flip side, there is also a very good chance that it can all backfire spectacularly, and then you are left with the worst of all decisions: how do you get rid of them?

Here's an idea for you...

Go through the interview process even if you are employing a relative or friend whom you have known for years. You will be able to explain the aims and objectives of the business and the ground rules regarding timekeeping, professional conduct and dress code in the manner in which you intend to run the business. Unless you actually tell someone what you expect of them, they will not deliver.

Make sure you are familiar with your rights and responsibilities as an employer before you hire anyone. In particular, write down clear, detailed job descriptions and give them to potential employees along with their contract of employment. The job description helps to focus everyone's attention on what is required, and can be very useful if there are subsequent disputes.

RECRUITMENT AGENCIES

Recruitment agencies perform a valuable service and expect to be paid accordingly. The charges vary wildly depending on your location, industry and the level at which the job is advertised. Using an agency often does result in your business being staffed by the right person, very quickly, but it comes at a cost. Don't feel any loyalty, advertise the role with as many agencies as possible, and take the position off their books if an agency continues to send unsuitable applicants.

WEBSITE

You really should have a website to both advertise and showcase your business. If there are services or products that can be sold via the internet, then you are probably doing this already. The moment that a vacancy for employment is on offer, it is always best to try and attract the right candidates yourself. Adding a jobs page to your site is incredibly cheap and can be highly effective.

ADVERTS

Placing adverts for positions vacant can be an
expense option, but if you are able to write
and place well-written adverts in well-targeted
locations, then the savings and quality of applicant can be very good indeed. The
level of the position will quickly make it obvious where you really need to be
advertising. Local papers do serve a function, but only really up to a certain level.
The national newspapers are expensive but their penetration, assuming you
research the paper's readership and themes, can prove to be one single payment
resulting in a plethora of interest, all from good candidates.

*'Furious activity is no
substitute for
understanding.'*
H.H. WILLIAMS, lawyer and author

Defining idea...

PRETTY TO LOOK AT, NOT MUCH GOOD

Don't be tempted to hire someone for their pretty/handsome face if you think his
or her skill set is lacking. Whilst for most of us it is nice to be surrounded by
beautiful people, at the end of the day you are employing staff to work for your
business, not give you an ego trip.

How did it go?

Q **We are so busy getting everything prepared for the launch it seems a bit counter-productive to timetable an interview. Can't this wait until we get a quiet moment in a few weeks' time?**

A *There are no quiet moments with new businesses and it really is unwise to hold an interview for the position weeks or months after someone has been working in the role. Just thirty minutes will do it and it's another tick on the list.*

Q **My cousin is notoriously bad at getting out of bed in the mornings but I know that once he gets into work he'll make up the hours. I don't want to rock the boat at this early stage and I need all the help I can get. What should I do?**

A *No other employer would tolerate late mornings; either he arrives on time for the working day (whatever those hours are) or he finds employment elsewhere. If you are lenient with one member of staff, it will strain relations with other members very quickly.*

Q **I have one very talented potential employee who wants to work from home most of the time. She says she doesn't need to come in more than one morning a week. What should I do?**

A *If you can agree on a way for measuring her output, why not let her organise things the ways she wants? As long as she does the work, does she really need to be in the office all the time?*

40

Keep up the good work

Some of your best career promoters are the members of your team. If they speak with pride of their department and warmly about you senior managers will notice. Replace someone who is running a happy team with great care. You've got to maintain performance and get them on your side.

You can't be a clone of your predecessor. Would you rather take over a team with a positive mental attitude or a bunch of demoralised grumblers? The former could be waiting for you to fail to live up to your glorious predecessor.

This happened to me when I took over a team from Martin, who had got himself a neat promotion after producing very good results and this very happy team.

Martin was a very quick thinker, he was also tactically bold and 100 per cent sure of himself – the perfect mixture for an autocratic manager. The team came to him for everything; no one else took decisions, not even small ones. I knew that I couldn't work like that. It wasn't my style, I didn't think it developed the individuals in the team – besides it looked like bloody hard work and by nature I'm a bit of a skiver.

When you take over a new job, watch out for the people who stay completely loyal to your predecessor and take every opportunity to rubbish you. They can have a huge impact on the team, particularly the junior and younger members, and they are almost certainly pouring poison into your boss's ear as well. This is a time to be ruthless. Get shot of them now. Don't wait for the rotten apple to spread the disease.

I thought about it long and hard and discussed the situation with one of my mentors; then I came up with a plan. In the first week I arranged to meet every member of the team individually for a 45-minute slot. During the quiet 15 minutes between appointments I read a newspaper and drank coffee. In that time, of course, the door opened several times and people asked me what to do in particular situations. I developed a catchphrase response, 'I don't know mate, I'm new here.' Eventually they got the idea and I developed a new culture where people came to me with solutions not problems.

'No man will make a great leader who wants to do it all himself, or to get all the credit for doing it.'
ANDREW CARNEGIE, industrialist

Luckily when I took over from Martin I was very careful to keep my boss up to speed. My new team really thrashed around. They looked and felt rudderless. Since I wasn't telling them what to do, they would go to my boss when I wasn't in. She handled it quite well but did give advice in some cases where I would have preferred her not to. She was concerned that what I was doing would impact performance, at least in the short term. Now, funnily enough, it didn't. Not sure why, although it is probably connected to the fact that the best people in the team quickly started to just get on with it and then they started to enjoy it, and the change had at least started.

Q **I've taken over a team of managers from one of the most respected, and I would say loved, members of the organisation. I can't do what you did because she ran a very consultative style anyway. The team is devastated. I'm struggling – do you have any advice on handling it?**

How did it go?

A *Blimey, are you sure this was a smart career move? At the moment I can only think of avoiding the threats. The biggest threat here is a so-called 'government in exile'. This happens when the person you took over from, particularly if you are the Chief Executive, holds regular government-in-exile board meetings. They gather all their best mates together for a social event and probably, in the nicest possible way, bitch about you like mad. Speak to your predecessor about it. Flatter her nauseatingly, really lay it on thick and ask her directly to keep her contacts with the team minimal. In fact, I think that is how I would deal with this situation. Ask her for advice; she knows the people well and will be able to help. I would also be inclined to bring at least one person you know into the team, and get rid of at least one of the original team. Then everyone knows that change is happening and that life will never be exactly the same again.*

How did it go?

Q **I am in the situation you describe. I'm all right with most of the team, but one of them won't change how they work. We agree how he is going to handle something and then I find that he has done something completely different. He always has brilliant reasons. It's starting to make me angry. Should I fire him?**

A *Not if he is good at his job and if the team like and respect him – or at least not yet. I am assuming that you are in quite a senior position. What about bringing in a deputy who is an old pal of yours? He can then supervise activities more closely and perhaps put in some business process that forces the man to change. Make sure the old pal is good with people, though. He has to get the rest of the team behind him.*

41

Lead with style

The ultimate test of leadership is the top job. As you progress in that direction you need the people above you and the people below you to admire the way you go about leading your team.

Good senior managers can smell a well-motivated, happy team from a mile off. The team members exude confidence. They work hard and make sacrifices.

They display pride in their work and in their membership of what they honestly believe is the best bit of the organisation. Not only that, but everyone, including Human Resources, will know that people are queuing up to get into that team. How do you create this aura?

Some say leaders are born and cannot be created, and it's true that your basic ability to get on with people is, to some extent, your starting point for being a leader. But there are a number of leadership techniques that develop your natural ability to make things happen. Think about motivation – leadership is the skill of persuading people to co-operate *willingly* to achieve results. The willingly is key: you cannot force motivation

Here's an idea for you...

At your next team meeting take the role of chairman absolutely seriously on at least one important topic. Do not make any proposals for possible actions yourself or appear to support any particular view. Let the team decide what to do, summarise their plan, and thank them for their hard work and good thinking.

on people; they have to want to do a good job. Motivation occurs when people feel that they're able to make their very best contribution.

DO YOU TELL 'EM OR SELL 'EM?

Some people talk about 'push and pull' management styles. Push is the 'do what you are told' or autocratic method; pull is the consulting, democratic way of leading people. You need a combination of the two for different people and in different situations.

Mike Brearley, sometime captain of the England cricket team, was reckoned to have 'a degree in people'. Here's an example told by Bob Willis, a fast bowler in Brearley's side. Willis was involved in Brearley's occasional winding up of the swashbuckling Ian Botham. When he felt that he needed to ginger Botham up, Brearley would signal to Willis, to take a message to Botham: 'Mike says that you're bowling like a girl.' Pity the poor batsman who faced the next ball from a seething Botham. Willis concluded this story by saying that if the captain had used the same words with him it would have destroyed his confidence and had the opposite effect. Useful things, degrees in people.

So, your team leadership style can range from giving simple directives to group discussion and consensus. If you tend too much towards giving directions you will, among other things, stifle the creativity of the team. That in turn reduces the number of times you will be able to take a good new idea to your boss. There is almost nothing that boosts a career more than being the first to make an innovative idea work and having it taken up by the rest of the company. Everybody will want to talk to you about it.

FINALLY

Always remember that people work for money but will do a bit extra for recognition, praise and reward. If you think someone is doing a good job don't forget to tell them. Show appreciation often. Don't wait for the end of a task to say thanks. It is often a good idea to thank someone in the middle of a project for getting on with it without having to involve you.

So, show a genuine interest in other people, communicate well and pick the right style at the right time and you will probably become a born leader and smell beautiful to senior managers.

Defining idea...

'You can play your role hands off if it works, but the opposite of hands off management is scruff of the neck management.'
ARTHUR WARD, a serial non-executive director of many companies

Defining idea...

'It was the nation and the race dwelling all round the globe that had the lion's heart. I had the luck to be called upon to give the roar.'
WINSTON CHURCHILL

How did it go?

Q **I tend to run my team with a vigorous push style and I have fallen into the trap of displaying the fact that I could do the job better than them. I have, after all, actually done all the jobs below me. I know that one of my guys is about to do something less than perfectly. What do I do? Just let him get on with it?**

A *Well yes, as long as it's not going to damage performance significantly. Let him do it his way. If it works in the end, what does it matter? If it goes wrong, he'll learn from the mistake. Eventually what will happen is that someone will do something differently to you and get a better result. You have to let the team develop if you want to smell of success.*

Q **I tried your idea about being the chair of a meeting and not making my views known. Next thing, the most senior member in the team takes over the proposing and leading role. How do you stop someone else stepping in to dominate proceedings?**

A *You could try briefing her on what you are trying to do before the event. If that doesn't work you must use what is called a 'labelled shut out'. You name the offender, and tell her you want to hear another named person out. Don't forget to bring the quietest members in to the discussion. You never know where the best ideas will come from.*

Q **This consensus stuff is for the birds. If the team is rushing around saying that they are coming up with all the ideas, won't I run the risk of looking like a weak leader?**

A *No, Adolf, you'll look like someone who gets the best out of their team.*

42

Show us what you can do

Two items that often come up in second interviews or assessment centres are in-tray exercises and presentations.

Don't let the time pressure rush you into rash decisions on the in-tray. Make sure you know your exact aim for your presentation.

They can simulate your in-tray very dramatically nowadays, with twenty emails in your inbox, your computer buzzing to signal an urgent message and a tray overflowing with paperwork.

BE SYSTEMATIC AND BE SEEN TO BE SYSTEMATIC

Don't act on the items as they come. Make sure you've read everything before you make any decisions. There could be a snake at the bottom of the pile. It's also likely that one item will have an impact on another. The most popular way of handling an in-tray exercise is, like all great techniques, very simple. Put the paperwork and emails into three categories – A, B, C – by assessing their urgency and impact.

Here's an idea for you...

It's a good idea to announce at the start of a role-play presentation exactly what you want the group to decide at the end. The audience then knows where you're going to take them. Some people avoid this, since there's a risk that someone in the audience will tell you it won't be possible to achieve your aim; but logically it is better to know this at the start of the presentation than at the end. If you know what the audience's objections are, you may be able to use the presentation to overcome them.

'Urgent' is something that's got to be done or it'll be too late. 'Impact' measures how much an item affects the profit-and-loss account or other people.

A: Stuff that you think is urgent, that in real life you would do today – things you're going to deal with during the exercise. Matters to do with customers are most likely to occupy this category.

B: Stuff that's important but not as urgent as A. You'll get round to these today only if you finish with A. Tomorrow these matters could well go into A.

C: Material that may still be important. You need to know where it is, so that if something happens that changes its urgency or impact you can promote the item to A or B.

If during the exercise they interrupt you with phone calls, establish quickly who is calling and what their position is. You'll want to speak immediately to your boss, for example, since they may well change at least one of your priorities. When these interruptions occur, make sure that an observer can see you're applying the same systematic rules to each one, and putting those that don't need action now into C, even when someone on the phone says the matter's urgent.

PRESENTATION TIPS

If you're not a natural at presentations, go on training until you can at least survive. We know one senior manager who made it to the top and remained a complete liability on his feet. When asked how he'd survived he replied, 'Ducking and weaving, old boy. I avoided presentations like the plague.'

The best tips for making effective presentations are the usual suspects: set tight objectives and talk exclusively in terms the audience will understand. The easiest way to set objectives for a presentation is to write down, 'At the end of this presentation the audience will:

- do something
- be able to do something
- have a certain attitude towards an event or plan.

This works well for an interview presentation and makes your preparation easier and quicker. In an interview, you will also have in mind the impression of you that you want to leave behind. For example: 'They'll see my drive and energy, my good listening skills and the fact that I work thoughtfully without making rash decisions.'

During your preparation, try to put yourself in the audience's shoes. This should help you to use only the language that they use and understand. Don't forget when you're planning your magnificent opening that you've also got to finish with a bang. (We've both found that 'Er, well, that's it' is a frequently used ending.) Allow time for questions and think through what the questions are likely to be, so you can

'*Unless one is a genius, it is best to aim at being intelligible.*'
SIR ANTHONY HOPE HOSKINS, British novelist

Defining idea...

respond professionally. Lots of good presentations founder at question time. Only cover the main points on the visual aids, make sure they have impact and don't just read them out. They're aids for you to talk round.

How did it go?

Q   I tried to do the ABC analysis but it went wrong. A lot of the in-tray was email. I tried to add the letters A, B or C on to the messages, but got confused and in the end missed a really important item. What should I have done?

A   *Either print out the emails or put the topic and a reference to the email on a piece of paper – or better a spreadsheet if you're quick at raising those. You can then sort the emails as you do everything else.*

Q   I was making a presentation to three people. Suddenly one of them made a point and another one bluntly disagreed with her. In no time they were at it hammer and tongs. I tried to break in, but in the end just looked like a raw prawn as I tried to get my voice heard. What were they doing?

A   *This is almost certainly a set-up to see if they can rattle you. Stop trying to present, look appealingly at the chairperson and, if they don't intervene, try, 'We've obviously got a disagreement here. Can I suggest that we move on and talk about that later on?'*

43

Be an achiever

An impressive job description doesn't necessarily mean you're good at what you do. Far more meaningful is a substantial record of personal achievements.

Shortly after Gerald Ford succeeded Richard Nixon, one commentator said of the impact Ford had made: 'A year ago, he was unknown throughout America, now he's unknown throughout the world.'

You may also have heard the Woody Allen line that 90% of success at work is about turning up. Perhaps that was true a while back, but these days that attitude won't achieve survival, let alone success.

Potential employers are interested in what you actually do and (more critically) what difference you actually make rather than in what you're supposed to do. A CV that simply sets out a mini job description for all the roles you've held is therefore missing a trick.

Here's an idea for you...

Rate thirty or so achievements in terms of the likely impact they'll have on a recruiter. Ask yourself which are the strongest examples and aim to use those rather than their weaker counterparts.

CVs have become increasingly achievement oriented in recent years. An achievement-based CV will give a potential employer a clear idea of the impact that you might have if recruited.

If you're planning to enter the job market in the near future you therefore need to be able to build into your CV an impressive set of achievements. By and large, though, we're pretty crap at recording our personal corporate triumphs. We tend to be a bit like one of those plucky British chaps in classic war movies who saves the entire regiment and then says in all modesty that he was only doing his job and there's no need to make a fuss as he still has one perfectly good leg left. In a similar way, we often don't give ourselves credit for the skills and abilities we have built up over the years and instead take them for granted.

Here's a quick exercise to help you see how good you are at recognising your achievements:

1. Write down thirty or so achievements that you're really proud of. If listing thirty achievements sounds excessive, please persevere. There's a tendency for people to do this exercise on automatic pilot to begin with. By the time you're up to achievement 23, you'll start surprising yourself with all you've done that had slipped from immediate recollection.

2. Alongside each achievement, make a note of the underlying skills or abilities you drew on in order to succeed.

> *'Do, or do not. There is no try.'*
> YODA, wise master of the Force and teacher of Jedi

Defining idea...

Armed with the output from this exercise, you should get a pretty good idea of the skills and abilities you can take into the job marketplace.

Bear in mind that achievements are contextual; in other words, our work environment and the corporate culture that we're part of shape what's expected of us and what's possible for us to achieve. For example, you may have the capacity to be innovative yet work in an environment that's unsupportive of innovation, such as a risk-averse life assurance company. You may therefore struggle to come up with a work-based example of being innovative. Where this is the case and where you're putting yourself forward for a role that requires innovative thinking, you may need to provide an achievement that drew on innovation from either a previous role or from a non-work situation. It's perfectly legitimate to use such examples in your CV.

The downside with achievements is that – like much of your CV – they have a shelf life. A genuine achievement that goes back ten years or more won't carry as much of an impact as a more recent example will. I'm reminded of a quote that was allegedly printed on clothing worn by Britney Spears: 'I'm a virgin, but this is an old T-shirt.' But come what may, you'll need a demonstrable record of achievements in order to achieve your career ambitions. Without it, your marketability will plummet.

> *'Always drink upstream from the herd.'*
> WILL ROGERS, American humorist and actor

Defining idea...

191

How did it go?

Q **Although I'm comfortable with expressing my work contribution in the form of achievement statements, how can I be sure these will match up with what my next employer (hopefully) is looking for?**

A *Sometimes we can be a bit literal in assessing the value of our achievements. Somebody selling encyclopedias door to door might focus on their sales figures, where they come in the sales league relative to colleagues and whether they've increased sales over the past year. Behind that performance there are a whole set of promotable skills. If the next employer (hopefully) is looking for characters with resilience, determination, self-motivation and good people skills, then it's perfectly possible that somebody selling encyclopedias could demonstrate those qualities extremely well.*

Q **I work in a very team-based environment so is it alright to concentrate on reporting team achievements?**

A *To a degree. Team-based achievements can indicate that you're a strong team player capable of working well with others. The trouble is that over-reliance on team-based content may obscure your individual contribution. Imagine you played in a football team and your team won the match 4–0. To a degree you could bathe in some reflected glory, but what if your sole contribution on the pitch was to concede a needless penalty, argue with the referee and get sent off after three minutes? That's why employers like to look behind team performance and get a glimpse of what you individually bring to the party. For that reason, do try to balance the team stuff with some of your personal attributes and strengths.*

44

Leave the office on time

Reduce interruptions. Reclaim your evenings.

Take control. Don't let your working day be hijacked by others. The secret is to have your goals clear in your mind.

THINK WEEKLY, THEN DAILY

Don't be a slave to a daily 'to-do' list. See the big picture. On Monday morning lose the sinking 'I've got so much to do' sensation. Instead, think 'What are my goals for this week?' Decide what you want to have done by Friday and then break each goal into smaller tasks that have to be undertaken to achieve all you want by Friday. Slot these tasks in throughout your week. This helps you prioritise so that the tricky and difficult things, or tasks that depend on other people's input, don't sink to the back of your consciousness. It also means you are giving attention to all that you have to do and not spending too much time on one task at the beginning of the week.

Concentrate on three or four items on your 'to-do' list at once. You won't be overwhelmed.

Here's an idea for you... **Create a 'virtual you' if you're getting stressed out in the office by the demands of others. When you're an administrative lynchpin, set up a shared file where people can go to find the information or resources they'd usually get from you.**

WORK WITH YOUR ENERGY CYCLES

Some of us operate better in the morning, some in the late afternoon. If your job demands creativity, block out your most creative periods so that you can concentrate on your projects. Don't allow them to be impinged upon by meetings and phone calls that could be done anytime.

Make the phone call you're dreading   Right now. That call that saps your energy all day. Just do it.

Have meetings in the morning   People are frisky. They want to whizz through stuff and get on with their day. Morning meetings go much faster than those scheduled in the afternoon.

Check emails three times a day   First thing in the morning, just after lunch and just before you leave are ideal times. Keeping to this discipline means that you don't use email as a distraction.

Limit phone calls   Talk to other people when it suits you, not them. In my working life I receive around twenty phone calls a day. Answer machines don't help me personally – the call-back list is another chore. This is how I turned it around. The most time-effective way of using the phone is to limit your calls as you do your emails – to three times a day. Make a list of calls you have to make that day. Call first thing. If someone isn't there, leave a message and unless you have to talk to them urgently, ask them to call you back at your next 'phone period'. Just before lunch is good. That means neither of you will linger over the call. Your other 'phone time' should be around 4.30 p.m. for the same reason. Of course, you can't limit phone calls completely to these times but most of us have some control over incoming calls. I don't have a secretary any more to screen calls, but I very politely say 'Sorry, I'm in the middle of something.' I tell the caller when I'll be free and most people offer to call me back then, saving me the hassle of calling them. No one minds that if their call isn't urgent. The point of all of this is to keep phone calls shorter by putting them in the context of a busy working day. Social chat is important and nice but most of us spend too much time on it. Time restrictions stop us rambling on. And this goes for personal calls too. Check your watch as soon a friend calls. Give yourself five minutes maximum. Or better still save personal calls as a treat for a hardworking morning.

'Take a note of the balls you're juggling. As you keep your work, health, family, friends and spirit in the air, remember that work is a rubber ball and will bounce back if you drop it. All the rest are made of glass; drop one of them and it will be irrevocably scuffed, tarnished or even smashed.'
JON BRIGGS, voice-over supremo

Defining idea...

How did it go?

Q **At the end of the day, I've worked really hard but have only done two things on my list. How can I avoid this soul-destroying feeling?**

A *Chances are you're an underestimator. Most of us are in this category. We seriously underestimate how long each job will take us, we fail to complete it – and so set ourselves up to feel ineffectual. Keeping a time log for a week, even better a month, gives you information on how long tasks really take you. Keep a detailed account of what you actually do half hour by half hour during the day for a week. This will give you facts. Deliver more than you promise and people will love you.*

Q **The culture in my office is that we stay late. Even if I got through my work, I'd have to stay. What's the answer?**

A *Different problem. At the end of the day (literally in this case), it's up to you. If you don't have family commitments, if you have a decent life–work balance, if your health is good, if you think the best use of your time is developing your career and MOST IMPORTANTLY if you think your hard work will be rewarded, then stay and work. But if not, then it might be time to rethink your priorities or find a new job.*

45

Ready, aim, fire

Keeping someone in your team who plainly is not going to make it can be very bad for your career. Your business performance suffers by definition and your boss sees you vacillating on an important issue, avoiding doing the right thing because it is uncomfortable.

Try not to create a dedicated enemy. Every manager has to sack someone from time to time. In fact some senior managers regard it as a key management skill. If you have to sack someone, timing is vital; but equally important is how you do it.

Don't forget how small a world the upper reaches of any industry are. You come across people whom you served as a customer, or for whom you worked, frequently enough for you to want to ensure that you only make enemies when there is no alternative. You may also come across people who worked for you in an earlier life, which means, of course, that you may come across people whom you fired.

Here's an idea for you... **Sometimes the Human Resources rules cause a hold-up. HR is, of course, quite right to protect the company's position and make sure that you do nothing that would prejudice that. But if the delay is going to cause problems, argue strongly that the company should buy its way out of it. This is often a time to spend the organisation's money lavishly.**

Sacking people is not a job that most managers find pleasant. Here are the dos and don'ts:

- Do prepare carefully, not only for the meeting but also for what will happen in personnel terms after it.

- Don't let the firee talk you out of it. If you've made your decision, stick to it. You will never recover with this person if you change your mind.

- Do have a stiff drink before the meeting. You need to look assertive, firm and friendly, not a nervous wreck.

- Don't relax too much. Jokes might not go down too well right now.

- Do give a generous if not lavish settlement. This sugars the pill greatly and if you go beyond the company's norms, the person you are firing will know that it is you being generous, not the rules.

- Do go through the process meticulously. It is important that it is you who gives the generous settlement not an industrial tribunal.

IT'S A JUNGLE OUT THERE:
TRY A HEADHUNTER

'*Never flinch – make up your own mind and do it.*'
MARGARET THATCHER

Defining idea...

Now's the time to consider the value of headhunters to your career. Headhunters are something else you should spend the organisation's money lavishly on – not difficult given what these guys charge. But they have an encyclopedic knowledge of your industry and the people and opportunities in it. They have to have; and they are very brazen about contacting people and keeping up to date. Perhaps you could help the person you are firing meet with a headhunter you know. That can sugar the pill. At the same time, encourage the headhunters to make suggestions to you at any time, not just when you want people or want a job for someone else. That way you are also encouraging them to do the same in terms of job opportunities for you.

Be very careful of the current fad for 'head-shunting'. This avoids the painful process of sacking someone by getting a headhunter to place a person you are trying to get rid of with another company. In theory, you avoid the expense of severance pay, and remove any threat of being sued for wrongful dismissal. But it would seem that someone who discovers that the ploy has been visited on them can still sue for unfair dismissal, and if the receiving company believes it has been duped, it also might have a case.

'*Aim high and achieve this by moving upwards between well-regarded organisations every two years.*'
P.R. WILLIAMS, HR Director, Vodafone Airtouch

Defining idea...

How did it go?

Q   **I finally bit the bullet and fired a guy, having put it off for about a year longer than I should. The problem is that while people knew he was not that good he was very likeable. Why has team morale gone south big time?**

A   *Team leadership jargon calls this 'grieving'. It happens when a team is reeling from a sudden change in personnel and will take a period of adjustment to get back on track. The danger here is that they will go back to an earlier stage in the building of the team and start to jockey for position and to struggle again to promote their individual ideas as the only way forward. You might choose to hold an event with a senior manager addressing the team and thanking them for their good work. That can have the impact of closure and moving on to the next phase without the person you fired.*

Q   **I've got to do it next week. My boss says that I should escort the person off the premises immediately. Is she right?**

A   *If there is a major security threat then, yes, she's right. But remember that you may come across the person again in your career, and this can look very brutal. I'm going to wimp out here and say that it depends on the situation and the person. Thinking back to two occasions when I did it, I got the first one to go directly because I knew they would go straight to a competitor. The other person I gave whatever time he wanted to work out his notice, or not. If I hadn't done that I believe the negative impact on my team would have been huge.*

46

Down to brass tacks

At some point in any interview you're going to have a somewhat technical discussion about the nitty-gritty of the job you're applying for. Make sure you get the detail right for the audience you're speaking to.

Interviewers want to hire interesting people who can steer clear of jargon when required, and display a personality that will contribute to the atmosphere of the working place. They don't want to hire crashing bores.

It's quite possible that someone, probably the potential line manager, will want to have a detailed technical discussion with you. If it's a one-on-one then that's fine. Go with the flow and enjoy talking to a fellow enthusiast. We're using this example to point out the pitfalls of such a discussion when other people, HR maybe or a senior manager, are also present.

Here's an idea for you...

Work out how to explain your job to a layperson in 100 words. Remember you've got to explain it in a way that shows that you have a wealth of knowledge and experience behind this simple statement which makes you a reliable resource to get the job done. Done that? OK, try it out on a few people. Teenagers are a good bet, since you can measure their concentration span in nanoseconds. When you've made that work, reduce it to fifty words.

FIND THE CONNECTION

You've got to say enough, of course, to prove that you have the technical ability to do the job. But leave any detail about that until after you've presented the answer in a way that shows the bridge between what your function is and how the organisation succeeds. We'll use the project management question to illustrate this idea, but it works for any function.

A project, or any department or function come to that, has its internal issues. You have to get the team to carry out the function and meet its objectives. But what outside managers are interested in is the interface where the project contributes to or harms the success of the organisation. They're also interested in the project when it impacts on other parts of the organisation. These are the bridges you're looking for when it comes to describing to non-technical people how you'll go about the job. In selling terms you're looking for the 'benefits' your function brings to the party.

So, 'At the outset I develop the objectives of the project and spend whatever time it takes to get all the stakeholders' agreement that we've got them right' is much better than, 'While not a perfect critical path analysis engine, Microsoft Project can be used to control the project and it has the benefit that most people are used to using it.'

Similarly, 'I'd talk to as many managers with relevant experience as possible to work out the resources we'd need during the project' is much better than, 'Once you've got the action plan the resource plan is quite straightforward. All you have to do is to reproduce the action plan as a resource plan.'

'A healthy male adult bore consumes each year one and a half times his weight in other people's patience.'
JOHN UPDIKE, US novelist

Defining idea...

KEEP IT VERY, VERY SIMPLE

The lurking snake in this type of question is the fact that you're probably going straight into your comfort zone. You've got the qualifications to do the job, you've had the training to do the job and you've got experience of doing the job; so it's a whole lot easier to spend time on this bit than on tricky questions about subjects such as managing difficult people or making sure the customer drives your strategic plan. So we go on and on and on.

There's another useful technique here to keep things simple. Give them the simplest possible explanation of how you manage a project. Then ask them if they want more detail. In this example it could be as simple as, 'Planning a project needs forward thinking: who and what do I need to get the job done? It also needs backward thinking: if it's got to be finished by the end of the year what needs to be done and when?'

How did
it go?

Q **I know exactly what you mean with this one. But what you're suggesting doesn't work. I had a very difficult time in my last interview with a technical person and her boss's boss. I tried to give 'bridge' type answers but every time she brought me back to the detail of what I did in my last job and what I would do if offered this job. I could see that the senior guy was losing interest: he was starting to read a report he'd taken out of his briefcase. How could I have stopped this?**

A *You've got to grasp the nettle here. Ask a question of the senior person like, 'Am I going into too much detail for you?' They may say, 'No, no, carry on.' In which case you do. Or they may decide to move on. Remember that all your competitors will have had the same problem and some will have happily gone into huge detail and completely turned the senior person off.*

Q **It's not possible to digest my complex job into 100 words let alone fifty. What am I supposed to do?**

A *Don't forget that politicians and generals only need the answer to six questions such as, 'Do we have enough fuel to carry out the campaign?' in order to decide whether to go to war or not.*

47

Handling rejection

**A rejection letter needn't be the end of the story.
A good follow-up strategy can keep you in the corporate
mind's eye.**

As one of my friends puts it, rejection is
life's way of saying 'Not yet'. Admittedly, my
friend has a very optimistic disposition, but
there are real benefits in not taking rejection
too hard.

Picture this scenario. You've had the interview. It seemed to go well and you came away thinking that you could enjoy working there. You go home and await the outcome of the interview only to be told that – stab my vitals – the organisation has opted to go for another candidate. At this point, you can adopt one of three dispositions:

1. Stoically take it on the chin and focus on the next application.

2. Unleash a volley of foul-mouthed bile to the effect that the interviewer and in fact the entire company should be dropped down a sizeable hole and forgotten about until the end of time.

205

Here's an idea for you...

Keep a record of every vacancy you apply for. When an application comes to the end of the road (for example, if you're not shortlisted or if you're interviewed but not offered the job), jot down a note of any lessons you've learned from that particular application.

3. Turn rejection into an opportunity to build something for the future.

The first two dispositions are both understandable at a human level, but they treat a rejection as the end of the road. The third disposition suggests that all may not be lost. Someone of the third disposition will recognise that success in the job search process is typically not about being head and shoulders above all other candidates – it's about striving to be a few per cent better than the competition every step of the way.

Examples of how to gain that advantage include: having a CV that conveys your experience and achievements more effectively; researching a company that bit more thoroughly; being that bit better prepared for the interview; making a better first impression at interview than others; and, critically in this context, following up key stages of the selection process more effectively than others. So, for example, when you get back home after an interview consider dropping a line to the interviewer to say that you enjoyed the interview and reconfirm your interest in the job. This is also your opportunity to enclose any information or material that you discussed at the interview and may have promised to provide.

If you're not offered a particular job, think seriously about asking for some feedback on your performance. You could also write to the interviewer(s). Perhaps send something along

'That which does not kill me makes me stronger.'
FRIEDRICH NIETZSCHE

Defining idea...

the lines of: 'Thank you for letting me know the outcome of my recent interview. Obviously I'm disappointed not to have been offered the job, as I would have greatly relished taking on this challenging and exciting role. I'd like to take this chance to reaffirm my genuine interest in your organisation and to ask you to bear me in mind for any suitable vacancies that might arise in the future.'

Gratuitous toadying? I don't think so. You're simply bringing this particular episode to a close whilst leaving channels of communication open. The organisation will think well of you for doing this and who knows what might come of it. Moreover, for a whole host of reasons the vacancy may reoccur. What if the candidate they offered the job to gets an even better offer from somewhere else or finds that the family don't want to relocate? If this happens, then obviously there are no guarantees, but at least you've left yourself well positioned for the organisation to come back to you.

207

How did it go?

Q **The job I wanted has been offered to another candidate who's accepted the position. Can you put a positive spin on that?**

A *I certainly can! Look, it's only natural to feel disappointed. These days, the typical selection process can often involve assessment centres and a number of interviews so the emotional investment can be high. But when all is said and done, you have a choice now. You can never speak to the company again or you can try to salvage something positive from the experience. A polite note thanking them for their interest in you and reinforcing your interest in them leaves your relationship with them on a good footing and you never know where that might lead.*

Q **Can you give an example of where that might lead?**

A *Imagine another candidate has accepted their offer. They then get a better offer from another organisation or decide not to turn up for duty. Or they decide after a little while that the job isn't for them and leave after six months. Or what if the company has a similar role that becomes available? In any of these cases, the organisation could turn to you without having to go through the whole rigmarole of another advertisement and recruitment process.*

48

Jump start your salary

Do you deserve a higher salary? Well of course you do. Let's look at tactics and techniques for making a persuasive case to your boss.

Doing nothing is rarely a good strategy when it comes to managing your personal finances. This is particularly true when it comes to the salary you receive. (If you're a person of independent means, then skip this section. Wage slaves, read on.)

Although we might fondly imagine that our natural talent and unstinting commitment and contribution will bring its own recognition and reward as surely as Day follows Doris, the more likely scenario is that you'll end up as some kind of overlooked organisational Gollum, driven to embitterment and quietly convinced that you've been diddled out of your rightful reward.

Here's an idea for you...

Be prepared to be flexible. If your boss accepts the validity of your case but pleads emptiness of the department piggybank, come back with something like 'Greg, I can see the problem so let's see what else we can do. Maybe I could have an extra week's holiday and a company car as an alternative.'

This particular response obviously works best if you have a boss called Greg. But it is worth bearing in mind that your salary is only one part of the total compensation package.

But if nobody knows how good you really are, why on earth would your company throw more money at you? The prerequisites for getting your salary increased are that (a) you are reasonably competent, and (b) you're well regarded by your employers. If these basic elements aren't in place right now, I'd point you towards another book in this series – *Cultivate a Cool Career.*

But taking these as read, here are some tips for negotiating your way to an optimal package. The first decision you'll have to make is, in the words of Joe Strummer, 'Should I stay or should I go?'

If you decide you want to stay where you are – for the time being at least – then you'll need to start gathering evidence that shows why you already deserve an increase. Perhaps you can make the case that some colleagues are getting more pay for doing the same work, or that others are getting more pay even though you do more work.

Before you fix a time to talk with your boss, make sure you know what you want out of your negotiation. This means having three figures in mind: your ideal salary (i.e. the most you dare ask for without alienating your boss), your bottom line (i.e. the lowest figure you'd settle for) and your realistic goal (i.e. the figure that you think you have a good chance of getting).

Armed with this information, prepare your case and book a meeting with your boss. Make sure you time the meeting to your best advantage. If you've only been with the company a few months, or if you've just made the mother of all cock-ups, hold off for the time being.

More precisely, go for a time of day which gives you a fighting chance of finding your boss receptive and in good humour (e.g. not immediately after they've come back from the weekly knackers-in-a-mangle meeting with the MD).

'Like jazz, communication is improvisational. Each time you communicate with another person, you're playing it by ear…Negotiation is a particularly high-stakes form of communication, one that requires the lightning-quick, informed responses and decisions that characterise the best improvisational music.'
DEBORAH M. KOLB

Defining idea…

When you go to the meeting, have all the facts and figures at your fingertips. Take along relevant reports, sales figures, performance stats and any other documents that support your case. It might even be worth putting together a supporting document to leave with your boss.

If there's nothing doing, don't despair. Career-wise, it might be an excellent time to position yourself for recognition when the money does become available again. You can ask for added responsibilities or a new job title. You're taking a risk, of course, that you might be working harder in the short term for the same pay, but you've bolstered your bargaining position down the line. If nothing comes through eventually, then, to be honest, I'd be looking for a new place to work.

Apropos of which, here are a few negotiating tip and wrinkles to deploy when you've been offered a position with a new company.

Defining
idea...

'For they can conquer who believe they can.'
JOHN DRYDEN

- Always aim to negotiate with the decision-maker rather than through intermediaries.

- It's always preferable to negotiate on the basis of having received a written offer. Not only will this help to prevent misunderstandings, but it also helps to depersonalise the situation if you are negotiating over a piece of paper. Remember that you are often dealing with somebody who could soon be your new boss. It pays not to antagonise them.

- Keep the tone of the negotiation positive by reaffirming your real interest in joining the company, by emphasising how pleased you were to receive the offer, and by looking forward to working with the new company – it's just a matter of clearing up a few contractual points to everybody's satisfaction.

- Try to give the company a few options to respond to rather than box yourself into a corner.

- Don't let the process drag on. Negotiate crisply and settle quickly.

By the way, if you decide to reject the job offer, keep it courteous and professional. Remember that the people you are dealing with are probably good networkers also. The last thing you want is to be bad-mouthed within your industry for buggering people about. For that reason, drop the company a line saying that you were pleased to have been offered the job, but that you regret that you can't accept the offer. Give your reasons why, thank them for taking the time to meet with you and wish them well with filling the post.

Q **I've set up the meeting, but how do I figure out what amount to ask for?**

How did it go?

A *The amount of money you can ask for depends on how much you think you are worth to your organisation. If, for example, you are the keeper of some important technical knowledge, or are a member of a critical project team, or if your work has contributed directly to the company's sales and profits in a measurable way, then you can readily demonstrate your value.*

Q **OK, I'm not in some high-paid corporate role. What can I do if I get paid an hourly rate?**

A *Actually it's often easier to negotiate when you're paid hourly. Why? Because an extra £1 an hour barely registers on a company's financial radar. From your perspective, it might be a 10–20 per cent rise. From their perspective, the sum involved is one that a business might sign off without a second thought.*

213

49

Did someone say something?

If you better your communication skills you'll also improve your relationships, enhance your performance at work and create more enjoyment in your social life.

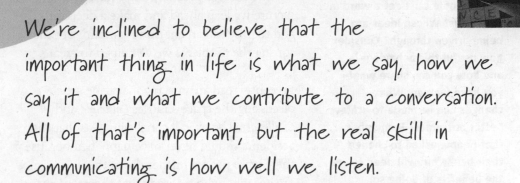

We're inclined to believe that the important thing in life is what we say, how we say it and what we contribute to a conversation. All of that's important, but the real skill in communicating is how well we listen.

LISTENING IS AN ART FORM

I used to find it virtually impossible to keep my mouth shut! Partly because I care passionately about people and I want to use the wisdom I've acquired from all my life experiences to help people. I was so excited that I hardly ever waited for people to finish their sentences before leaping in with my thoughts. Teaching personal leadership showed me that many people do the same thing, often for the best reasons in the world. When I finally truly learned about the power of listening, I was shocked beyond belief at how I'd continually interrupted others and not listened. I'd always thought that I was a good listener!

Here's an idea for you...

At your next meeting or family discussion, listen to people and don't interrupt. Observe what's happening. How much real listening is going on? What opportunities are being missed due to interruptions? How many people can't get a word in edgeways? Whose ideas are being driven through? Consider how useful this behaviour is and how you can share what you have learned. What changes can be made to achieve better outcomes? Remember that people asked to change their behaviour will need to see the benefits of doing so.

It's crazy because we'd like to be sure that we're making the best decisions possible in all aspects of our lives. How can we possibly do this if we never let people finish their sentences? Unless we listen to people, we won't fully understand what they're saying. Often when we probably don't have the full picture we leap ahead and make a decision, and then spend an enormous amount of time sorting the problems we've helped to create.

I recently read an amazing magazine article discussing the space shuttles *Columbia* and *Challenger*. The overall conclusion was that the accidents should never have happened because there were people further down the organisation who realised what the problems were. However, nobody was listening to them.

THE YELLOW BRICK ROAD

Imagine that you're walking down a yellow brick road to get to a beautiful castle. You can't see the castle clearly because it's hidden by mist, but you know you really want to get there and explore it. While you're walking, you meet a large group of people who you think will pass either side of you. They don't. They knock you over, trample all over you and kick you. Once they've gone, you get up and start heading towards the castle again. Soon you meet two great friends. They're going off on another path and, after lots of chat, persuade you to go with them before you go to the castle. You enjoy your trip with them but then return to the path to where you wanted to go in the first place – the castle. Next, you meet someone who knows exactly where you're going and doesn't want you to go there. That

'The reason we have two ears and only one mouth is that we may listen the more and talk the less.'
ZENO, Greek philosopher

Defining
idea...

person becomes violent and eventually drags you off to somewhere else. In reality, if there had been some police officers standing around they may well have arrested some of those people for physical violence.

Now imagine this scenario. You're in a meeting and you have an idea that isn't totally clear but you want to share it nevertheless. However, every time you try to open your mouth you find that everyone else is so busy talking about their ideas that you can't get a word in edgeways. Or they want you to look at their ideas first. Or you're told that your idea can't be considered because a decision has already been made.

What is the difference between these two pictures? I would like to suggest that there isn't one. One is physical violence; the other is mental. Every time you interrupt someone else it is in fact mental violence.

How did
it go?

Q   **At a meeting of the local cricket club I simply observed as you suggested. Nobody really listened to anyone else and there were non-stop interruptions. This helped me to understand my frustration with the group – we make such slow progress and have great difficulty making decisions. I know it'll happen again next time. What can I do?**

A   *Before the next meeting talk to some or all of the group about it. See if you can get at least one ally to support you in suggesting that the group really concentrates on listening. At the meeting explain the impact of interrupting and perhaps get everyone to point out when someone does it. Make it fun rather than criticising and you may be surprised at how much more effective and enjoyable the meeting is. Another way to avoid interrupting is to have an object such as a ball and only allow the person who is holding the ball to speak. And if someone with a bad case of verbal diarrhoea won't let the ball go, they'll learn fast because no one will pass the ball back to them!*

Q   **I've worked hard at this with my team at work. We're now so conscious of interrupting that the conversation is riddled with people apologising when they do it. Does it always remain so artificial?**

A   *No. Eventually the team will internalise its listening skills and the conversation will become less jerky. Listening is actually a 'learned' skill, and like anything we learn it takes time and practice to become more natural. So don't worry if this very conscious listening continues for a while, as it's far better than the alternative.*

50

How do I look?

Like it or not, your appearance and your health are of more and more interest to your employer. Think about what you look like and whether you are paying enough attention to fitness.

Are you fit for the purpose? It does, of course, depend. If your boss is a fitness freak you have a choice of two courses of action. Either you can join her and beat the hell out of your colleagues at squash or tennis or whatever, or you can religiously avoid exercise of all sorts. The latter makes a definite point, so think about it.

Nowadays there are myriad ways of keeping fit by working out before or after office hours. If you are a bit anti-exercise, which you probably are if you are reading this Idea, look carefully at all the opportunities. You don't have to do circuit training on a daily basis to give the impression that your health is as important to you as it is to

Here's an idea for you...

It is never a good idea in career terms to fail at anything, so don't try and do too much. For example, try using a personal trainer just once a week or twice a month. That should spur you to some effort. It will eventually be embarrassing to tell them week after week that you haven't been off the sofa since you last met.

your company. Walking can do it; so can cycling, jogging or roller-skating. If, however, your only exercise is straining to get the cork out of the bottle and the occasional one-night stand, you could follow nutritionist Nigel Bentley's advice and get off the bus or the tube a few stops early and walk the rest of the way. If that doesn't suit you, try sitting on a horse. That's a fine way to get some fresh air, good exercise and, for goodness' sake, a bit of excitement – you're quite high up off the ground. I've found that a bit of horse riding woke me up in the morning brilliantly and was as good a cure for a hangover as any.

If there are sports facilities at work use them by all means, but don't make a big thing about it. A lot of people, maybe most people, eventually find doing gym exercises monotonous and boring. So don't make yourself a hostage to fortune by shouting off about going to the gym every day after work; your bosses will notice when you stop.

A colleague of mine, Tony, tells the story of his personal trainer. Tony is a man who could eat for his country. He puts as much passion into eating and drinking as he does into his pretty successful career. The price he pays is a weight problem. At appraisal time his boss seemed to make light of it when he said, 'What about shedding a bit of weight, Tony, we don't want to lose you to a heart attack.' Tony realised that there was more to the comment than light-hearted banter, so he hired a personal trainer. The woman took her job as a trainer very seriously and went through a detailed questionnaire on Tony's lifestyle and dietary habits. Each item was scored and at the end of the questions she totted up Tony's total, read the possible outcomes and finally announced in a puzzled voice that according to her charts he was already dead.

'This is the Law of the Yukon, that only the Strong shall thrive;
That surely the Weak shall perish, and only the Fit survive.'
ROBERT W. SERVICE, Canadian poet

Defining idea...

WHAT DO YOUR CLOTHES SAY?

The advice of one of the senior telecommunications people I have trained is not for the faint hearted. He says that you should avoid looking like everyone else. If the first thing board members know about you is that you wear bow ties, you have made your point. Some of them may not like it, but this is compensated for by the fact that they've noticed you. I was always a little nervous about the topic of appearance in my one-on-one coaching sessions with senior managers. In the end I decided that the right question to ask yourself is whether your clothes are saying what you want them to say. Back to the telecommunications man. He always wore eccentric clothes – green corduroy suits featured heavily, along with brightly coloured braces and ties. In the nature of the training course I had to ask the question, 'What do you think your clothes say about you?' He responded, 'They say that although I have got a senior job in your organisation, you will never own me.' I couldn't argue with that.

How did it go?

Q **I started to enjoy getting fit when they put a gym into the basement. But the people who do it tend to be the strong silent types and I've lost touch with a valuable grapevine I used to be plugged into. How do I keep up with, or in with, the people I used to gossip with in the pub after work?**

A *Ah, you are trying to run with the fox and ride with the hounds, an excellent idea in career terms. Never mind a foot in both camps, what you want is one in each tent. Take a night off the treadmill at least once a week for god's sake. You're trying to become Mr Chairman, not Mr Universe.*

Q **My boss looks like an unmade bed and emits a definite pong. You should see the funny looks he gets from our customers. Should I tell him?**

A *Noooo. It's much too dangerous. Get someone else to tell him. Probably best is your Human Resources contact, or if you are feeling brave, your boss's boss. Be warned: I once talked to a delegate about her appearance in a one-on-one coaching session. She took the hump with me and it did me no good at all.*

51

Know thyself

Self-assessment is hard. Either we are unfair on ourselves and are unwilling to give ourselves credit or we blow our own horn a bit too much. It's time for some objectivity.

Be fair to yourself and to others when assessing individual worth; if you get it wrong, your colleagues are likely to become extremely upset.

You might regard yourself as ideal for your role and ideal for running your own business, and you may well be right, but it is always worthwhile treating yourself (just for a few minutes) as a stranger. If you met yourself, how would you describe that meeting? If your answers include loving, adorable, and a great guy, you're probably not taking the exercise particularly seriously. Understanding what skills you hold, and more importantly, what your weaknesses are, will quickly determine what skill sets the business needs to employ to make the venture a success. Do not ignore the fact that you are not particularly strong at certain aspects of running a business – not everyone is an effective communicator, or negotiator, or happy to sit typing invoices. To pretend to yourself and others that you can do absolutely everything required by the business is foolhardy.

Here's an idea for you...

Write out, in full, the job description when you are recruiting. Now write down the core competencies of that role in two sections, 'need to have' and 'nice to have'. By explaining your requirements, your vacancy will not only be more attractive to the people best-suited for the job, but will minimise the number of no-hopers applying for the role.

DIRECTORS WITHOUT PORTFOLIOS

A very clever way to make your business appear successful and well organised, along with filling any gaps in your and the other directors' skill sets, is to organise a skills audit. This exercise determines what skills are held within the company and exposes any gaps or weaknesses. Ask everyone to list their own skills, giving details, and identifying areas of weakness. Explain that honesty is essential, and that the information will not be held against them – it is simply to help the company discover what skills it has and what it lacks.

The answer to these shortfalls is to find non-executive directors or less-formal business partners from outside of the business to act in the company's best interest. It is often the case that directors of a business all come from a similar background or industry. In many ways this is ideal – you have a number of individuals who are all very experienced in the trade that the company is intending to offer. Having said that, if all your staff have similar backgrounds, you will find that skills overlap and there remain some gaps – more often than not in the Finance Department, unless you all happen to be accountants setting up a new venture. It is wise to secure the assistance of someone prepared to act as a director of finance. You will quickly find that those persons looking after the cash of a business will identify all the projects that sound wonderful but will eventually turn out to be unprofitable. A good director of finance will save you a fortune.

'If you're going to be a healer, it's not enough to read books and learn allegorical stories. You need to get your feet wet, get some clinical experience under your belt.'
DIANE FROLOY and ANDREW SCHNEIDER, screenwriters

Defining idea...

CHOOSING YOUR FRIENDS

Assessing the skills of others does not stop at the recruitment and employment of the directors of the business; it must carry right down to the rank and file of the business and be foremost in your mind when you are hiring staff. Always prepare well for interviews and be absolutely clear in your mind what you are looking for in each candidate. If the role you are looking to fill requires a good working knowledge of computers and specific software packages, do not be tempted to hire someone who promises to learn – find the candidate who fits the vacancy, do not alter the role to fit the candidate.

How did
it go?

Q **I am not planning on taking on a member of staff until the business is eighteen months old and financially established. Can't this exercise wait?**

A *If you are planning to take on a member of staff, ever, then create the job description now, when your mind is still full of ideas from writing the business plan and discussing the business every hour of every day. You will be in a stronger position to write the description now. It can always be finalised nearer the time.*

Q **What is the significance of the 'nice to haves'?**

A *Hopefully, when the job is advertised you will attract only suitable candidates. Having a number of 'nice to haves' will allow you to choose 'a first among equals' because they will have not only satisfied the core competencies but also bring extra skills or experience (or a very attractive list of contacts) to the role.*

Q **I'm having trouble getting people to assess their own skills. What should I do?**

A *Try doing it in group sessions, using a white board. Explain what is needed, and then write down your own skills and shortcomings on the board. Depending on the group, you can then ask everyone to complete their own assessment on paper while you wait, or you can laboriously drag the information out of each person and write it on the white board – this may take more time, but may be necessary if the individuals are not used to this kind of work. Make sure someone keeps a record, though!*

52

Face it, you are you and they are them

Take a positive, practical but sceptical attitude to your organisation. Don't expect to spend your whole career in one organisation and don't trip over internal politics.

Are you in the right place? People are happier and work better when they can identify with the objectives of the organisation they work for.

It is hard to get up in the morning with energy and enthusiasm if you feel that your work contributes to something you couldn't care less about. Make sure you are working for an organisation that is doing something worthwhile and is likely to be successful. You are much more likely to build a career there.

If right now you're working towards a goal that neither interests you nor inspires you, you've got to make a change. It's up to you. Your career is a key element in your way of life and your general happiness; if you are in the wrong place get out of it.

It is best for your boss to think that other people believe your good ideas are his. You, on the other hand, should ensure people know that your ideas and your boss's good ideas are both yours.

YOU HAVE OUR UNDIVIDED LOYALTY

until it doesn't suit us

Now let's look at the other side of the coin – the organisation itself. Your organisation is probably chaotic, either all the time, or sometimes, or in places. This is both a problem and an opportunity for the career minded. This chaos means that whatever it says about looking after you and your career, your company may very well not be able to live up to its promises. Organisations, for example, have to take technological change on board if they are to survive even if it costs careers. In short, the organisation has to look after itself in a businesslike way, so you need to look after yourself in a similarly objective and professional way.

And circumstances change. A promise made to a member of staff in good faith may suddenly become impractical. In this environment the safest view to take of your organisation is that you owe it your loyal support only for as long as your objectives and the organisation's can co-exist. Career planning is now a question of a number of jobs rather than a simple progression up a single organisation. Companies don't offer jobs for life and most successful careerists will change employers from time to time. Keep an open mind and don't get so set in your ways that you get caught out by a reorganisation in which you find yourself 'Co-ordinator of Long-term Planning'. Such a post almost certainly means that you are no longer part of those long-term plans. I'm certainly not encouraging you to be dishonest yourself. But be warned that others are sometimes going to use 'their best intentions' to meet their obligations.

Defining idea...

'Success has many fathers, failure is an orphan.'

Career players take integrity very seriously. They do not, however, ignore the facts of the new world – the company man is extinct. The key phrase now is 'fluidity of labour'.

NURTURE THE POLITICIAN WITHIN YOU

It is not possible for any organisation to exist without some form of internal politics. People often have conflicting agendas and objectives. Face it. Don't make a decision on behalf of an organisation without paying attention to what the implications are for you. If company politics permeate every decision that affects your career, you should face another brutal fact: *in company politics the competition is your colleagues.* After all, this is more than a matter of survival. The Vicar of Bray played his organisation's politics well and survived, but he never made it to bishop. My Dad, watching the politics that my mother got into in a small local church, was heard to murmur, 'The more I see of Christians, the more sorry I feel for the lions.' If the Church cannot avoid internal politics and strife, what chance has a capitalist corporation?

'Except in poker, bridge and similar play period activities: don't con anybody. Not your spouse, not your children, not your employees, not your customers, not your stockholders, not your boss, not your associates, not your suppliers, not your regulatory authorities, not even your competitors.'
ROBERT TOWNSEND, Avis CEO

Defining idea…

FINALLY

So, it's a question of 'us and them', or rather, remembering what we have said about your colleagues, of 'me and them'. Take responsibility for your own career, and work on the basis that no one else will.

How did it go?

Q **I have started to look at my colleagues as the enemy in career terms. It is tending to make me avoid contact with them in less guarded situations like over lunch or drink after work. Is this right?**

A *No. Such gatherings are an important source of information – and you need to know your enemy. These occasions also often present opportunities to do a bit of internal politicking. Just make sure you obey the salesperson's mantra – you must tell the truth and nothing but the truth, but show me someone who tells the whole truth and I'll show you a loser.*

Q **My new boss says that there are no politics in our part of the organisation and he doesn't want any to start.**

A *He's lying.*

Q **I hate company politics; it is energy sapping and wastes time. Do I have to think about them at all?**

A *I think you do. Have a look at the successful people around you. You will find they all talk about and think about their and other people's positions and abilities.*

The end...

Or is it a new beginning? We hope that the ideas in this book will have inspired you to try some new things to boost your career prospects. You've discovered that by making a little bit of effort here and changing a few priorities there your working life is starting to pick up. Hopefully the tips you read here will help to get you noticed by the right people and talked about for the right reasons.

So why not let *us* know all about it? Tell us how you got on. What did it for you – what really made you flavour of the office? Maybe you've got some tips of your own you want to share (see next page if so). And if you liked this book you may find we have even more brilliant ideas that could change other areas of your life for the better.

You'll find the Infinite Ideas crew waiting for you online at www.infideas.com.

Or if you prefer to write, then send your letters to:
The best value career book ever
The Infinite Ideas Company Ltd
36 St Giles, Oxford OX1 3LD, United Kingdom

We want to know what you think, because we're all working on making our lives better too. Give us your feedback and you could win a copy of another *52 Brilliant Ideas* book of your choice. Or maybe get a crack at writing your own.

Good luck. Be brilliant.

Offer one

CASH IN YOUR IDEAS

We hope you enjoy this book. We hope it inspires, amuses, educates and entertains you. But we don't assume that you're a novice, or that this is the first book that you've bought on the subject. You've got ideas of your own. Maybe our author has missed an idea that you use successfully. If so, why not send it to yourauthormissedatrick@infideas.com, and if we like it we'll post it on our bulletin board. Better still, if your idea makes it into print we'll send you four books of your choice or the cash equivalent. You'll be fully credited so that everyone knows you've had another Brilliant Idea.

Offer two

HOW COULD YOU REFUSE?

Amazing discounts on bulk quantities of Infinite Ideas books are available to corporations, professional associations and other organisations.

For details call us on:
+44 (0)1865 514888
Fax: +44 (0)1865 514777
or e-mail: info@infideas.com

Where it's at...

brilliant ideas

The Best Value Ever Series is published by Infinite Ideas, publishers of the acclaimed **52 Brilliant Ideas** series and a range of other titles which are all life-enhancing and entertaining. If you found this book of interest, you may want to take advantage of this special offer. Choose any two books from the selection below and you'll get one of them free of charge*. See p. 240 for prices and details on how to place your order.

Goddess
Be the woman YOU want to be Edited by Elisabeth Wilson
BUMPER BOOK – CONTAINS 149 IDEAS!

Healthy cooking for Children
52 brilliant ideas to dump the junk
By Mandy Francis

Adventure sports
52 brilliant ideas for taking yourself to the limit
By Steve Shipside

Skiing and snowboarding
52 brilliant ideas for fun on the slopes
By Cathy Struthers

Getting away with it
Shortcuts to the things you don't really deserve
Compiled by Steve Shipside

Re-energise your sex life (2nd edition)
52 brilliant ideas to put the zing back into your lovemaking
By Elisabeth Wilson

Stress proof your life
52 brilliant ideas for taking control
By Elisabeth Wilson

Upgrade your brain
52 brilliant ideas for everyday genius
By John Middleton

Inspired creative writing
Secrets of the master wordsmiths
By Alexander Gordon Smith

Detox your finances
Secrets of personal finance success
By John Middleton

Unleash your creativity
Secrets of creative genius
By Rob Bevan &
Tim Wright

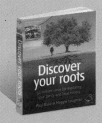

Discover your roots
52 brilliant ideas for exploring your family & local history
By Paul Blake &
Maggie Loughran

For more detailed information on these books and others published by Infinite Ideas please visit www.infideas.com

The best value career book ever

Choose any two titles from below and receive the cheapest one free.

Qty	Title	RRP
	Goddess	£18.99
	Healthy cooking for children	£12.99
	Adventure sports	£12.99
	Skiing and snowboarding	£12.99
	Getting away with it	£6.99
	Re-energise your sex life (2ND EDITION)	£12.99
	Stress proof your life	£12.99
	Upgrade your brain	£12.99
	Inspired creative writing	£12.99
	Unleash your creativity	£12.99
	Detox your finances	£12.99
	Discover your roots	£12.99
Subtract lowest priced book if ordering two titles		
Add £2.75 postage per delivery address		
Final TOTAL		

Name: ....

Delivery address: ....

....

....

....

E-mail:...Tel (in case of problems): ....

By post Fill in all relevant details, cut out or photocopy this page and send along with a cheque made payable to Infinite Ideas. Send to: Best Value Offer, Infinite Ideas, 36 St Giles, Oxford OX1 3LD, UK.

Credit card orders over the telephone Call +44 (0) 1865 514 888. Lines are open 9am to 5pm Monday to Friday. Just mention the promotion code 'BVAD06.'

Please note that no payment will be processed until your order has been dispatched. Goods are dispatched through Royal Mail within 14 working days, when in stock. We never forward personal details on to third parties or bombard you with junk mail. This offer is valid for UK and RoI residents only. Any questions or comments please contact us on 01865 514 888 or email info@infideas.com.